cooking
vegetables

MURDOCH BOOKS

contents

The new life that bursts forth in spring includes some of the sweetest and crispest of all vegetables. Treat them to brief and simple cooking methods to keep them at their lively best.

This is the season of maturity and abundance, of fresh salads and quick, easy dishes that are big on flavour and short on preparation, so you can make the most of the long, hot days.

The growing world begins to slow down now, but still produces culinary treasures aplenty. Versatile autumn vegetables shine in substantial, sumptuous and filling dishes.

Slow-cooked meals bring out the best in winter's tubers, root vegetables and hardy leafy greens, sustaining and nourishing both body and soul and brightening the dark days of the year.

a delicious seasonal bounty

Poor old vegetables suffer from an unfortunate image problem. Heavily pushed as being good for us, there is an unspoken assumption that eating them is a necessary yet unpleasant chore. Generations of mothers have felt compelled to insist that there will be no ice-cream until the broccoli is eaten. Sadly, many of us don't discover a taste for vegetables until we're adults. By avoiding vegetables, we are not just depriving ourselves of the health-giving nutrients they contain, but also of the life-enhancing pleasure of eating them, and enjoying the range of amazing flavours, uses and 'mouth-feel' that they offer.

There is no cuisine that does not rest on a foundation of vegetables. While many of us think of protein as the main event and vegetables as something to go on the side, this is a recent development, allowed only by intensive farming and supermarket convenience. For most of history, meat and fish were an unpredictable luxury and vegetables, fruit and grains — those things that we could grow for ourselves — were the staples that kept us alive.

Before the refrigerator, diet was inevitably dictated by the seasons, the harvest, climate and location; we ate what we could grow and made the most of what we had. Now, air-freight and cold storage provide a level of convenience and choice that would have been unimaginable to the home cook of an earlier age. Dining on strawberries mid-winter or peas all year round would have been the preserve of the immensely wealthy, or simply impossible. We may have gained a luxury, but we have lost something much richer — a connection to our food and a real sense of place. Travel around much of Asia or southern Europe and what you will still find is a cuisine that isn't so much national as regional. While the basics may be similar, the detail of each dish will reflect the particular ingredients at hand as the dish was created. From valley to valley, the micro-climate changes; the clever gardener plants what will thrive, so the basket of fresh vegetables collected for each meal is unique to its place.

Food plays an odd role in our lives. It is so necessary, so intrinsic as to be somehow below consideration, and yet its role in the global firmament is inescapable. Food represents love, nurturing and memory; it keeps us alive and makes us feel alive; it has driven history and defined entire populations; and sitting at the base of the food tree, holding everything else up, are vegetables. So next time you peel a potato or shuck an ear of corn, remember, you're not just making dinner; you are creating memories, sustaining life and taking your place in a richly textured tapestry of home cooks and the food they create.

spring

Spring is a time of new beginnings. There's a vital urgency in the air, a smell of nature bursting back to life in all its soft, green glory. The freshness of spring reawakens the physical and sensual, reconnecting us to senses that have lain dormant throughout the winter months. Instead of long, slow meals that fill us up and keep us warm, we want snap, crackle and pop. Rather than vegetables simmered to a yielding softness, we want to feel that bite of spring on our palate as well as in the air. The move away from the sustaining root vegetables to tender, sweet baby greens is as natural as the growing seasons themselves.

At the first sign of spring, market gardens and fields explode into new, green life. Pea vines are laden with fat, juicy pods full of sweet, green peas. Beans of every variety, but especially broad beans, are at their tender, lively best. The first crop of tender asparagus is pushing its way through the soil to the light. Fresh herbs are back on the menu, thriving wherever they are planted.

Plenty is not the only gift of spring; it also heralds the return of variety and quality. Both markets and supermarkets offer an almost bewildering array of tempting goodies to choose from. You may find yourself lugging home such a pile of fresh produce that it's difficult to cook and eat it all before it is past its best. The essence of spring is the freshness of its offerings, the brand-spanking newness of it all. Capture this by shopping selectively and often; look for a local market, make use of your local grocer, let the experts do the sourcing for you. Buying little and often reconnects us to an earlier time when we stocked our table with the fruits of our own labour. Meals were made with what could be picked fresh from the garden, and profligacy was a luxury afforded to the few.

Beyond the benefits of crispness and flavour, truly fresh food offers a range of vitamins and minerals that no tablet could ever hope to imitate. There's no quicker way to health than stocking your house with the best seasonal food. And by supporting your local greengrocer, you get the added bonus of keeping your local community alive with choice and variety.

Simplicity is the only rule in making the most of spring vegetables. Clean, crisp flavours are best achieved by taking a light approach with both method and seasoning. Rather than treating the vegetables as a background for other foods, look for simple ways to enhance their natural sweetness and crisp vitality. Purity of flavour and a delicious variety of fresh, baby produce are the great gifts of generous, bountiful spring.

asparagus and prawn pizzetta .... makes 4

ASPARAGUS AND PRAWNS (SHRIMP) ARE ONE OF THOSE PERFECT, UNIVERSALLY APPEALING FLAVOUR COMBINATIONS. AND WHO SAID THAT MAKING PIZZA BASES AT HOME WAS A WASTE OF TIME? THIS STRAIGHT-FORWARD METHOD COULDN'T BE EASIER, AND IT GIVES A CRISP CRUST WITH PLENTY OF FLAVOUR.

pizza dough

caster (superfine) sugar	1 teaspoon
active dried yeast	1 teaspoon
plain (all-purpose) flour	225 g (8 oz/1¾ cups)
olive oil	60 ml (2 fl oz/¼ cup)
olive oil spray	for coating
mozzarella cheese	110 g (3¾ oz/¾ cup) grated
pecorino pepato cheese	50 g (1¾ oz/½ cup) finely grated
raw medium prawns (shrimp)	300 g (10½ oz), peeled and deveined
basil	1 large handful
olive oil	1½ tablespoons
asparagus	12 thin spears, trimmed, halved on the diagonal
spring onions (scallions)	4, white part only, thinly sliced on the diagonal
baby English spinach leaves	1 small handful, trimmed
extra virgin olive oil	1–2 tablespoons

To make the pizza dough, put the sugar, yeast and 2 tablespoons warm water in a small bowl and stir until dissolved. Leave in a warm, draught-free place for 10 minutes or until bubbles appear on the surface. The mixture should be frothy and slightly increased in volume. If your yeast doesn't froth it is dead, and you will have to discard it and start again.

Sift the flour and ¼ teaspoon salt in a large bowl. Make a well in the centre and add the oil, 60 ml (2 fl oz/¼ cup) warm water and the yeast mixture. Mix with a wooden spoon until the mixture clumps together in a rough dough.

Transfer the dough to a lightly floured surface and knead into a ball. The dough should be soft and moist, but not sticking to your hands. If necessary, knead in a little flour or warm water. Knead the dough for 5 minutes, then lightly spray with olive oil spray and put it in a clean bowl. Cover with plastic wrap, then a tea towel, and set aside in a warm, draught-free place for 1 hour.

Preheat the oven to 210°C (415°F/Gas 6–7). Lightly grease 2 large baking sheets. Divide the dough into 4 portions. Shape each into a ball with your hands, then roll it out to a 15 cm (6 inch) circle. Transfer to the baking sheets and set aside for 5 minutes.

Scatter the mozzarella over each pizzetta, leaving a 1 cm (½ inch) border. Scatter the pecorino pepato over the mozzarella, followed by the prawns and half the basil. Brush the edge of the dough with a little olive oil. Season the pizzettas well with salt and freshly ground black pepper and drizzle with the remaining olive oil. Bake for 15 minutes, or until the dough is crisp and golden.

Meanwhile, bring a large saucepan of water to the boil. Add the asparagus and cook for 2 minutes, then drain. Combine the asparagus with the spring onion, spinach and remaining basil. Season with salt and freshly ground black pepper. Scatter the asparagus mixture over each cooked pizzetta and drizzle with extra virgin olive oil.

warm salad of watercress, citrus and spring lamb

THIS SALAD IS SPRING ON A PLATE: THE ZING OF CITRUS COMBINES WITH THE PEPPERY, MUSTARDY TASTE OF RAW WATERCRESS LEAVES TO COMPLEMENT SEARED LAMB. FOR THE TENDEREST RESULTS, TRY SPRING LAMB (3–10 MONTHS OLD) OR MILK-FED LAMB (GENERALLY UNDER 8 WEEKS OF AGE).

dressing

red wine vinegar	1 tablespoon
garlic	1 clove, crushed
honey	1/2 teaspoon
walnut oil	2 teaspoons
olive oil	1 1/2 tablespoons
lamb fillets	300 g (10 1/2 oz)
olive oil	1 tablespoon
oranges	2
pink grapefruit	1 small
watercress	3 large handfuls, picked over
red onion	1/2 small, finely sliced

To make the dressing, put all the ingredients in a small bowl, season with salt and freshly ground black pepper and whisk to combine.

Cut the lamb fillets in half and season with freshly ground black pepper. Heat the olive oil in a frying pan over high heat and cook the lamb for 3–4 minutes, or until browned, turning once or twice. Season with salt and remove from the heat.

Peel the oranges and grapefruit, removing all the white pith. Holding them over a bowl to catch the juice, segment them by using a small, sharp knife to cut between the membranes. Put the segments in the bowl with the juices.

Cut the lamb on the diagonal into 2.5 cm (1 inch) thick slices and add to the bowl, along with the watercress and red onion. Pour the dressing over the salad and lightly toss to coat.

Too often, watercress is seen as nothing more than a garnish. While its dainty form and deep, luscious colour are certainly decorative, the powerful little leaves of this aquatic plant have a versatility and impact that belie their fragile appearance. Using watercress is a simple way to bring a complex, peppery edge to a dish without disturbing the delicate balance of flavours. Like most dark green, leafy vegetables, watercress is an excellent source of iron. Fresh is always best, so try growing your own. As with any type of cress, it must be washed thoroughly before use. Buy dark leaves with no yellowing and use quickly. To store, stand stems in a bowl of water, cover with a plastic bag and refrigerate.

chargrilled asparagus and chicken .... serves 4

ASPARAGUS COOKS BEAUTIFULLY ON THE CHARGRILL. ITS FLAVOUR IS INTENSIFIED AND IT TENDS TO STAY CRISP AND BRIGHT. MANY BELIEVE THAT THE BIGGEST BENEFIT IS IN THE TIMING — WHERE A MATTER OF SECONDS CAN BE CRITICAL WHEN STEAMING OR BOILING, GRILLING OFFERS A LOT MORE LEEWAY.

dressing

oil	80 ml (2¹/₂ fl oz/¹/₃ cup)
coconut milk	2 tablespoons
lime juice	2 teaspoons
makrut (kaffir lime) zest	1 teaspoon grated
garlic	2 cloves, crushed
mint	¹/₂ teaspoon finely chopped
chicken tenderloins	6 medium (about 225 g/8 oz)
asparagus	16 spears, trimmed
oil spray	for cooking
small mint leaves	1 handful
long green chilli	¹/₂, seeded and finely shredded

To make the dressing, put half the oil, the coconut milk, lime juice, lime zest and garlic in a small bowl and season with a little salt and plenty of freshly ground black pepper. Mix well.

Trim the white sinew from the thick end of the chicken tenderloins and halve them lengthways. Put the chicken and asparagus spears in a shallow non-metallic dish. Pour in half the dressing and toss to coat. Set aside to marinate for 30 minutes. Add the remaining oil and the mint to the other half of the dressing.

Spray a hot barbecue plate or chargrill pan with oil. Remove the asparagus and chicken from the marinade, drain and cook for 7–8 minutes, or until browned and cooked through, turning the asparagus often and the chicken once. Discard the marinade.

Transfer the asparagus and chicken to a bowl, add the mint leaves and chilli and toss lightly. Pile in the centre of 4 plates and drizzle with the dressing. Serve warm or at room temperature.

With a sharp knife, cut the chicken tenderloins in half

Marinate the chicken strips and the asparagus in the dressing

Chargrill until browned and cooked through

chokos with cashews and coconut milk

.... serves 4

CHOKOS (CHAYOTES) ARE NATIVE TO TROPICAL AMERICA, AND WERE EATEN BY THE AZTEC AND MAYAN PEOPLES. HERE, THEIR DELICATE FLAVOUR IS SPICED UP BY THE ADDITION OF INGREDIENTS COMMON TO THE COOKING OF SOUTHERN INDIA — COCONUT MILK, CURRY LEAVES AND CASHEWS.

raw cashew nuts	150 g (5½ oz/1 cup)
vegetable oil	2 tablespoons
onion	1, finely sliced
garlic	2 cloves, crushed
turmeric	1 teaspoon ground
cinnamon	1 stick
curry leaves	8
coconut milk	400 ml (14 fl oz)
chokos (chayotes)	4 small
Thai basil	small handful
steamed white rice	to serve

Soak the cashews in water overnight. Drain and dry on paper towels. Finely chop half of the cashews by hand or in a food processor and reserve. Heat the oil in a saucepan and add the whole cashews. Fry over medium–low heat until golden. Remove with a slotted spoon and reserve.

Add the onion and garlic to the pan and fry until softened, about 5 minutes, then add the turmeric, cinnamon stick and curry leaves. Cook, stirring often, for 2 minutes. Add the coconut milk and 350 ml (12 fl oz) water. Bring slowly to the boil then simmer for 5 minutes.

Peel the chokos and cut each into 4 wedges. Discard the seed and slice the flesh into chunks. Add to the pan and return the mixture to a simmer. Stir through the chopped cashews and basil, remove from the heat and allow to rest for 2–3 minutes before serving. Serve with steamed rice.

Chokos (chayotes) are the green, pear-shaped fruits of a climbing vine. The firm white flesh, which tastes like a cross between apple and cucumber, surrounds a single inedible seed. The skin may be smooth or prickly. Chokos are easy to grow, but have fallen from fashion's favour. Luckily there is a small but growing fan-club dedicated to restoring these fruits to their rightful place in the culinary world. Chokos are easy to cook, but the trick is to treat them as a base and go to town on the seasoning. They may be boiled, baked, fried or stuffed, and used in either savoury or sweet dishes. Cook until just tender, but still with a bit of bite. Peel them under running water, as the skin secretes a sticky substance.

three ways with peas

FRESH PEAS ARE LITTLE GEMS OF SWEET GOODNESS. PEAS ALSO FREEZE VERY WELL, WHICH MEANS THAT THEY ARE AVAILABLE ALL YEAR ROUND, AND THEIR GENTLE FLAVOUR MAKES THEM EXTREMELY VERSATILE. STUDDED THROUGH A SPICY SAMOSA, THEY ADD A BURST OF COOL SWEETNESS TO EACH MOUTHFUL. MUSHY PEAS ARE CLASSIC NURSERY FOOD, BUT IT'S EASY TO MAKE THEM FRESH AND SOPHISTICATED WITH THE GENTLE ANISEED NOTE OF FENNEL. RISI E BISI, AN ITALIAN CLASSIC, PAIRS PEAS AND RICE FOR THE ULTIMATE IN COMFORT FOOD.

pea and potato samosas

Blend 30 g (1 oz) ghee with 200 g (7 oz/1¾ cups) plain (all-purpose) flour in a food processor until combined. Add a large pinch of salt and 100 ml (3½ fl oz) warm water and process until the dough forms a ball. Knead 4–5 times, then cover and chill for 30 minutes. Shell 200 g (7 oz) peas to give 70 g (2½ oz/½ cup). Cook the peas in boiling water until just tender, then drain. Heat 20 g (¾ oz) ghee in a frying pan over medium heat. Fry ½ finely chopped small onion, 85 g (3 oz/½ cup) diced potato, 2 crushed garlic cloves, 2 teaspoons each of grated fresh ginger and garam masala, ½ teaspoon each of ground cumin and ground coriander, and ¼ teaspoon each of turmeric and chilli powder for 5–6 minutes, stirring often. Stir in the cooked peas. Roll out the dough to 1 mm (1/16 inch) thick and cut out ten 10 cm (4 inch) rounds. Put some of the pea mixture in the centre of each round and brush the edges with water. Fold over the pastry to enclose the filling and press the edges well to seal. Fill a deep-fryer, wok or heavy-based saucepan one-third full of vegetable oil and heat to 180°C (350°F) or until a cube of bread dropped into the oil browns in 15 seconds. Deep-fry the samosas in the oil until browned, about 2 minutes. Serve with 250 g (9 oz/1 cup) plain yoghurt mixed with 2 teaspoons chopped mint and ¼ teaspoon each of ground coriander and ground cumin. Makes 10.

mushy peas with fennel and spring onions

Shell 850 g (1 lb 14 oz) peas to give 320 g (11¼ oz/2 cups). Peel 1 small potato and cut into 2 cm (¾ inch) cubes. Heat 20 g (¾ oz) butter and 1 tablespoon oil in a large saucepan over medium–low heat and fry 1 thinly sliced baby fennel bulb for 3–4 minutes, or until soft. Add the peas, potato, 250 ml (9 fl oz/1 cup) milk and enough water to just cover the vegetables. Simmer for about 15 minutes, until the peas and potato are tender and the liquid has evaporated. Stir regularly towards the end of the cooking time to prevent sticking. Season with salt, pepper and a good pinch of ground nutmeg. Add 4 thinly sliced spring onions (scallions) and 1 small handful chopped fennel leaves. Roughly break up the mixture using a potato masher or fork. Serve hot, drizzled with extra virgin olive oil. Serves 4.

risi e bisi

Shell 800 g (1 lb 12 oz) peas to give 300 g (10½ oz/2 cups). Heat 1 litre (35 fl oz/4 cups) chicken stock in a saucepan. Heat 55 g (2 oz) butter in a large, deep frying pan over low heat. Fry 6 sliced spring onions (scallions) and 1 chopped middle bacon slice for 3 minutes. Add 325 g (11½ oz/1½ cups) arborio rice and stir to coat. Add a ladleful of hot stock and simmer until it is almost absorbed. Add the peas and another ladleful of stock and cook until the stock is almost absorbed. Continue in this way until the rice is tender but *al dente*. This will take 15–20 minutes. There should still be enough liquid in the pan for it to flow. Stir through 30 g (1 oz) butter and 50 g (1¾ oz/½ cup) shredded parmesan cheese. Season with salt and freshly ground black pepper and set aside for 1 minute before serving. Serves 4.

watercress and green pea sauce on mahi-mahi fillets

.... serves 4

BOTH PRODUCTS OF THE SUNNY DAYS OF SPRING, WATERCRESS AND PEAS COMBINE TO GIVE A FRESH-TASTING, SLIGHTLY SWEET SAUCE THAT GOES PARTICULARLY WELL WITH SEAFOOD. ADD SOME OF THE DELICATE WATERCRESS STEMS WHEN PICKING OVER THE BUNCH, AND THROW A COUPLE OF PEA PODS INTO THE POT, TOO.

sauce

butter	15 g (1/2 oz)
leek	1 small, white part only, thinly sliced
dried mint	1/4 teaspoon
shelled peas	100 g (31/2 oz / 3/4 cup)
chicken stock	2 tablespoons
watercress	50 g (13/4 oz) leaves and tops of stems, chopped
cayenne pepper	a pinch
crème fraîche	2 tablespoons
olive oil spray	for cooking
mahi-mahi fillets	4 (or other firm white fish fillets)
plain (all-purpose) flour	for dusting
watercress	250 g (9 oz / 1/2 bunch), leaves and tips only
red onion	1/2 small, thinly sliced
pistachio kernels	35 g (11/4 oz / 1/4 cup) coarsely chopped

To make the watercress sauce, heat the butter in a medium frying pan over low heat and fry the leek for 5 minutes without browning. Add the mint and peas, cook for 1 minute and then add the stock. Bring to the boil, then reduce the heat and simmer for 5 minutes.

Stir in the watercress, increase the heat and simmer for 2 minutes, or until the liquid has evaporated. Add the cayenne and season with salt and pepper. Transfer to a food processor or blender and purée the sauce until very smooth. Return to the cleaned saucepan, stir in the crème fraîche and keep warm over low heat. If necessary, stir in hot water, 1 teaspoon at a time, to maintain a thin mayonnaise consistency.

Spray a hot chargrill pan with olive oil. Lightly dust the fish with flour and season with salt and freshly ground white pepper. Cook until opaque, 4–5 minutes each side, depending on the thickness of the fillets.

Make a bed of watercress on each serving plate. Scatter the red onion and pistachios over and around the watercress. Top with a fish fillet and spoon a dollop of sauce on each. Serve hot.

Stir the watercress into the pea and leek mixture

Dust the fish fillets with plain (all-purpose) flour

fettuccine primavera with
smoked salmon .... serves 4

IN ITALY, PASTA PRIMAVERA HERALDS THE ARRIVAL OF SPRINGTIME. THIS VARIATION COMBINES YOUNG RUNNER
BEANS, ASPARAGUS AND SNOW PEAS (MANGETOUT) — THE BEST OF GREEN SPRING VEGETABLES — IN A LIGHT,
CREAMY SAUCE. SMOKED SALMON ADDS A LUSH RICHNESS.

smoked salmon	100 g (3½ oz) sliced
young runner beans	125 g (4½ oz)
asparagus	12 spears, trimmed
snow peas (mangetout)	60 g (2¼ oz), topped and tailed
fettuccine	350 g (12 oz)
crème fraîche	250 g (9 oz/1 cup)
cream	125 ml (4 fl oz/½ cup)
lime zest	1 teaspoon finely grated
basil	1 small handful, torn if large

Cut the smoked salmon into 2 x 5 cm (³/₄ x 2 inch) strips.

Halve the beans on the diagonal. Cut the asparagus into 4 cm (1½ inch) lengths. Slice the snow peas on the diagonal. Bring a large saucepan of salted water to the boil. Add the beans, simmer for 2 minutes, then add the asparagus and simmer for 2 minutes more. Add the snow peas during the last 30 seconds of cooking. Remove all the vegetables from the pan using a slotted spoon.

Return the water to the boil and cook the fettuccine until *al dente*.

Meanwhile, combine the crème fraîche and cream in a small saucepan. Season well with salt and freshly ground black pepper and bring to the boil. Simmer for 2 minutes, then reduce the heat to low. Add the lime zest.

Drain the pasta and return it to the pan. Add the cream mixture, salmon, basil and vegetables, toss to coat and serve immediately.

Snow peas (mangetout) are one of the true treats of the spring harvest. Their crisp, watery bite makes them the perfect foil to tender chicken in a light spring salad. Or make the most of their supple freshness in a stir-fry. For something different, add them to a curry right at the end; they'll retain just a little bite, yet still be soft and tender and absorb the juices wonderfully. There are two types: those with a flat thin pod (snow peas), and those with a more rounded pod (sugar snap or snap peas). Both types are best when perfectly fresh; they are not really designed to be stored at all. Left to linger in the fridge, they will quickly wilt, so for best results, buy them on the day you plan to use them. Top and tail them before cooking.

artichokes roasted with prosciutto, olives and anchovies . . . . serves 4

THIS CAN BE SERVED AS A SIDE DISH OR A LIGHT LUNCH, AND USES A CLASSIC COMBINATION OF FLAVOURS. SERVE IT HOT, OR SET IT ASIDE TO COOL AND ENJOY IT AT ROOM TEMPERATURE.

lemons	2, halved
globe artichokes	4, quartered lengthways, chokes removed
olive oil	2 tablespoons
dry white wine	250 ml (9 fl oz/1 cup)
lemon thyme	4 sprigs
garlic	1 clove, thinly sliced
niçoise or ligurian olives	40 g (1 1/2 oz/1/3 cup)
prosciutto	85 g (3 oz), thinly sliced
anchovy fillets	4, cut lengthways into 3 slices
extra virgin olive oil	to serve

Prepare the acidulated water and the artichokes according to the method on page 47, up to the cooking stage.

Preheat the oven to 190°C (375°F/Gas 5). Bring a large non-aluminium saucepan of water to the boil. Squeeze in the juice from the remaining lemon half, then add the lemon half. Add the artichokes, 2 teaspoons of the olive oil and 1/2 teaspoon salt. Put a plate on top of the artichokes to keep them submerged. Simmer for 12 minutes, then drain. Transfer the artichokes to a large shallow ceramic baking dish and pour over the wine and remaining olive oil. Scatter with the lemon thyme, garlic and olives. Cover with the prosciutto slices and bake for 30 minutes, or until the prosciutto and the tips of the artichokes start to crisp around the edges.

Transfer to a serving plate, breaking up the prosciutto and discarding any pieces that are too charred. Scatter the remaining prosciutto and the anchovies over the artichokes. Toss lightly and serve drizzled with olive oil.

three ways with asparagus

FOR THE TRUE FOOD LOVER, THE COMING OF SPRING IS HERALDED BY THE FIRST, SLENDER STALKS OF ASPARAGUS. SOME PREFER ASPARAGUS *AL DENTE*, BUT THE SOFTNESS OF WELL-COOKED STEMS PAIRS DIVINELY WITH GOAT'S CHEESE IN A TASTY TART. HOLLANDAISE SAUCE IS THE CLASSIC ACCOMPANIMENT FOR STEAMED ASPARAGUS; THE ADDITION OF TENDER, SALTY STRIPS OF PROSCUITTO RENDERS THE DISH SUBLIME. AND EGG AND ASPARAGUS ALWAYS GO WELL TOGETHER, AS IN THIS ASPARAGUS AND SPRING ONION FRITTATA.

asparagus and goat's cheese tart

Layer 2 sheets of shortcrust (pie) pastry on top of one another, roll out to a rough 30 cm (12 inch) circle and use to line a greased 23 cm (9 inch) loose-based tart tin. Trim the edges, prick the base with a fork and chill for 20 minutes. Line the pastry with crumpled baking paper, fill with baking weights or dried beans and bake blind in a preheated 200°C (400°F/Gas 6) oven for 20 minutes. Remove the weights and paper and bake for a further 15 minutes. Reduce the oven temperature to 190°C (375°F/Gas 5) and put a baking tray on the middle shelf of the oven. Peel 350 g (12 oz) thick white asparagus spears and cut off the tips at 6–8 cm (2½–3¼ inches). Blanch the tips in a large saucepan of boiling salted water for 3 minutes. Remove with a slotted spoon and set aside. Simmer the lower stalks for 4 minutes. Drain, roughly chop the stalks and process in a food processor with 3 eggs and 300 ml (10½ fl oz) cream (whipping). Season with salt and pepper and stir through the finely sliced white part of 4 spring onions (scallions) and 1 tablespoon thyme. Pour into the pastry shell. Scatter the asparagus tips and 60 g (2¼ oz/⅓ cup) crumbled goat's cheese over the filling. Bake on the baking tray for 35–45 minutes, or until puffed and golden. Serve warm or cold. Serves 4 to 6.

asparagus with prosciutto and hollandaise sauce

Whisk together 1 egg yolk and 1 teaspoon each of water, lemon juice and white wine vinegar and put in the top of a double boiler over simmering water, making sure it does not touch the water. Whisk for 1 minute, or until thick and foaming. Slowly pour in 60 ml (2 fl oz/¼ cup) melted unsalted butter, whisking constantly. Continue whisking for about 1 minute, until thick and creamy, then season with salt and pepper. Put 20 trimmed asparagus spears in a steamer basket over simmering water. Cover and steam until *al dente* (4–8 minutes, depending on the size and age of the asparagus). Group the asparagus into 4 bundles. Cut 1 slice of prosciutto into 4 long strips. Cook under a hot grill (broiler) until just starting to bubble. Wrap a strip of prosciutto around the middle of each asparagus bundle. Serve with the hollandaise sauce spooned over the bundles. Serves 4.

asparagus and spring onion frittata

Trim and halve 500 g (1 lb 2 oz) asparagus spears. Thinly slice the lower stalks, keeping the tips whole. Blanch all of the asparagus in boiling salted water until *al dente*, 2–4 minutes, then drain. Whisk 8 eggs, 35 g (1¼ oz/⅓ cup) grated parmesan cheese, 60 ml (2 fl oz/¼ cup) cream, 1 tablespoon plain (all-purpose) flour, a pinch of grated nutmeg and some salt and freshly ground black pepper in a bowl. Stir in the sliced asparagus, 4 sliced spring onions (scallions) and 1 teaspoon chopped thyme. Heat 2 teaspoons olive oil and 10 g (¼ oz) butter in a 20 cm (8 inch) non-stick frying pan and pour in the egg mixture. Cook over medium–low heat for 15–18 minutes, or until the egg begins to set and the base is golden. Scatter the asparagus tips and 55 g (2 oz) crumbled goat's cheese over the egg mixture. Cook until the edge is set, then cook under a preheated hot grill (broiler) until the top is set and golden brown. Serves 4 to 6.

asparagus and goat's cheese tart

fresh spring rolls with bok choy and snowpeas .... makes 8

FUN TO MAKE, WITH A MINIMUM OF COOKING, THESE FRESH SPRING ROLLS CAN BE PREPARED 2–3 HOURS IN ADVANCE AND LEFT AT ROOM TEMPERATURE, COVERED WITH DAMP PAPER TOWELS. ALTERNATIVELY, SET OUT SMALL BOWLS OF EACH INGREDIENT ON THE TABLE AND LET DINERS ASSEMBLE THEIR OWN.

dipping sauce

fish sauce	1 tablespoon
palm sugar	1 teaspoon grated
lime juice	1 tablespoon
coriander (cilantro) leaves	2 tablespoons finely chopped
red bird's eye chilli	1, finely chopped
dried rice vermicelli	50 g (1³/4 oz)
spring onions (scallions)	2
snow peas (mangetout)	30 g (1 oz), topped and tailed
Lebanese (short) cucumber	1/2
baby bok choy (pak choy)	2 (about 150 g/5¹/2 oz)
oil	1 tablespoon
garlic	1 clove, crushed
fresh ginger	1/2 teaspoon finely grated
round rice paper wrappers	8, each 16 cm (6¹/4 inches) in diameter
bean sprouts	30 g (1 oz/¹/3 cup), tailed
coriander (cilantro) leaves	1 small handful
hoisin sauce	60 ml (2 fl oz/¹/4 cup)

To make the dipping sauce, combine the fish sauce, palm sugar, lime juice and 2 tablespoons water in a small bow . Stir until the sugar has dissolved. Add the coriander and chilli and set aside.

Soak the vermicelli in hot water for 10 minutes, then drain.

Cut the spring onions into 7–8 cm (2³/4–3¹/4 inch) lengths and shred them lengthways. Shred the snow peas lengthways. Cut the cucumber into 7–8 cm (2³/4–3¹/4 inch) matchsticks.

Discard the outer leaves of the bok choy. Cut off the bases and separate the leaves. Heat the oil in a wok over medium–high heat and fry the garlic and ginger for 10–15 seconds, until aromatic. Add the bok choy and stir-fry for 20–30 seconds, or until wilted. Remove from the heat and cut lengthways into thin slices.

Soak a rice paper wrapper in lukewarm water just until soft. Spread a dry tea towel on a work surface and put the rice paper wrapper on top. Arrange a small bunch of vermicelli on one side. Top with 3–4 lengths of bok choy. Cover with 2–3 bean sprouts, slightly protruding over the rim of the wrapper. Add 2–3 snow pea strips, some spring onion and some cucumber sticks. Put 2 coriander leaves on top and spoon a thin trail of hoisin sauce along the length of the vegetables.

Fold the bottom of the wrapper up over the vegetables, then roll the wrapper up tightly from one side to give a firm cigar shape with a few vegetable sprigs sticking out the top. Repeat with the remaining ingredients to make 8 rolls. Serve with dipping sauce.

Spoon a drizzle of hoisin sauce over the vegetables

Fold up the bottom of the rice paper wrapper, then the sides

laksa with snake beans, chicken and seafood..serves 4

SNAKE OR YARD-LONG BEANS, AVAILABLE IN BUNCHES FROM ASIAN GREENGROCERS, CARRY HOT AND SPICY FLAVOURS WELL. THEY ARE AT THEIR BEST WHEN FIRM AND BRIGHT GREEN, AND THEY SHOULD SNAP WHEN BROKEN. AVOID BUNCHES THAT LOOK DULL AND LIMP, AND BEANS THAT FEEL SOFT AND HOLLOW.

raw medium prawns (shrimp)	250 g (9 oz)
snake (yard-long) beans	200 g (7 oz)
mung bean vermicelli	200 g (7 oz)
vegetable oil	1 tablespoon
chicken breast fillet	150 g (5½ oz), trimmed, cut into strips
firm white fish fillets	150 g (5½ oz), cut into 2 cm (¾ inch) cubes
Malaysian laksa paste	200 g (7 oz)
coconut cream	400 ml (14 fl oz)
makrut (kaffir lime) leaves	2, shredded
fish sauce	1–2 tablespoons
snow peas (mangetout)	50 g (1¾ oz), topped and tailed, shredded
spring onions (scallions)	2, thinly sliced on the diagonal
Vietnamese mint	1 small handful, torn
bean sprouts	50 g (1¾ oz/½ cup)
fried shallots	to serve (see note)

Peel and devein the prawns and put the heads and shells in a medium heavy-based saucepan over medium heat. Cook, turning often with a wooden spoon, for 6–8 minutes, until aromatic and dry. The pan will brown a little, but avoid allowing it to burn. Add 250 ml (9 fl oz/1 cup) water, bring to the boil, then reduce the heat and simmer until almost evaporated. Add another 250 ml (9 fl oz/1 cup) water and bring to the boil. Add 750 ml (26 fl oz/3 cups) water, return to the boil, then reduce the heat to low and simmer gently for 20–25 minutes. Strain and reserve the stock, discarding the shells. Measure the stock; you will need 500 ml (17 fl oz/2 cups). If you have less, add water.

Cut the snake beans into 8 cm (3¼ inch) lengths and slice them lengthways into quarters (or halves, if very thin). Put the beans in a large bowl, add the vermicelli and cover with boiling water.

Heat the oil in a large wok over medium heat and add the prawns, chicken and fish. Gently fry for 2–3 minutes, or until opaque. Remove from the wok. Add the laksa paste to the wok and cook, stirring, for 1 minute. Add the prawn stock, coconut cream, makrut leaves and fish sauce, to taste. Bring to the boil, then reduce the heat and simmer for 6 minutes.

Drain the noodles and beans. Reserve about a quarter of the beans. Divide the remaining beans and the noodles among 4 bowls. Top with the snow peas, spring onion, prawns, chicken, fish and half the mint. Ladle the hot stock into the bowls. Pile the bean sprouts and remaining beans and mint on top, and sprinkle with some fried shallots. Serve immediately.

Note: Fried shallots are available in jars from Asian supermarkets.

three ways with green beans

FROM THE SINUOUS CURVES OF SNAKE BEANS TO SOFT, PLUMP BROAD BEANS, SPRING IS A BOUNTEOUS SEASON FOR LOVERS OF THESE LEGUMES. FOR A SOFT, SATISFYING SIDE DISH SIDE WITH A DIFFERENCE, ROAST BABY BROAD BEANS WITH ARTICHOKES AND OLIVES. BEAUTIFUL, CRISP FRENCH BEANS ARE A VITAL INGREDIENT IN A CLASSIC NICOISE SALAD — TAKE THEM AWAY AND IT'S REALLY JUST A TUNA SALAD. THEIR FLAVOUR IS ALSO DIVINE SIMPLY STEAMED AND SERVED WITH SLIVERS OF NUTTY ALMONDS AND A TANGY MUSTARD DRESSING.

sautéed baby beans with artichokes and green olives

Blanch 200 g (7 oz) baby beans in boiling salted water for 2 minutes, then drain. Trim 8 spring onions (scallions) to roughly the same length as the beans. Heat 1 tablespoon olive oil in a large frying pan over medium heat. Sauté the beans, spring onions and 6 rosemary sprigs for 1–2 minutes, or until lightly browned. Remove from the heat. Add 85 g (3 oz/½ cup) green olives, 2 quartered artichoke hearts in brine, 1 tablespoon rinsed salted baby capers, 1 tablespoon extra virgin olive oil and 2 teaspoons tarragon vinegar. Season with salt and freshly ground black pepper and toss to coat the vegetables with the oil and vinegar. Pile in a dish and serve warm or at room temperature. Serves 4.

niçoise salad with french beans and seared tuna

Whisk together 80 ml (2½ fl oz/⅓ cup) olive oil, 2 crushed garlic cloves, 1 teaspoon dijon mustard and 1 tablespoon Champagne vinegar. Season well. Brush two 150 g (5½ oz) pieces of sashimi-quality tuna with olive oil. Fry on a hot barbecue or chargrill pan until browned, about 1½–2 minutes each side. Remove from the heat. Top and tail 225 g (8 oz) French beans and cook in boiling salted water for 3 minutes, or until just tender. Remove with tongs and drain. Scrub 450 g (1 lb) baby potatoes, cut in half and add to the saucepan. Boil for 12 minutes, or until tender. Drain and put in a shallow salad bowl with 2 large handfuls torn green lettuce leaves. Add 2 tablespoons of the dressing and toss gently to coat. Scatter 8 halved cherry tomatoes on top. Slice the tuna diagonally into 5 mm (¼ inch) slices and arrange on the tomatoes. Add the cooked beans and 12 niçoise or black olives. Cut 2 hard-boiled eggs into wedges and add to the salad. Arrange 4 halved anchovy fillets in a cross on top. Top with 1 tablespoon rinsed salted capers and drizzle with the remaining dressing. Serves 4.

snake beans and almonds with green peppercorn dressing

Cut 250 g (9 oz) snake (yard-long) beans into 10–12 cm (4–4½ inch) lengths. Cook in boiling salted water for 2–4 minutes, or until just tender. Drain and put in a serving dish. Dry-fry 85 g (3 oz/½ cup) blanched almonds in a small frying pan over medium heat for 2–4 minutes, or until coloured. Add to the beans. Crush 1 tablespoon drained green peppercorns to the consistency of coarsely ground black pepper. Whisk with 1 tablespoon each of olive oil, almond oil, lemon juice and dijon mustard. Season with salt, to taste. Pour the mixture over the beans and toss well. Serve hot or cold. Serves 4.

sauteed baby beans with artichokes and green olives

broad bean, smoked chicken and pesto salad

.... serves 4

THE COLOUR AND FRESHNESS OF BROAD (FAVA) BEANS AND PISTACHIO PESTO: SPRING ON A PLATE. THERE WILL BE SOME PESTO LEFT OVER. SPOON IT INTO A SEALABLE CONTAINER AND POUR A THIN LAYER OF OLIVE OIL OVER THE TOP. SEAL THE CONTAINER AND REFRIGERATE THE PESTO FOR UP TO 10 DAYS.

pistachio pesto

basil	1 small handful
rocket (arugula)	100 g (3½ oz/1 small bunch), picked over to give 30 g (1 oz)
parmesan cheese	2 tablespoons grated
garlic	1 clove
pistachio kernels	25 g (1 oz/¼ cup), roasted
olive oil	60 ml (2 fl oz/¼ cup)
cream (whipping)	2 tablespoons
broad (fava) beans	700 g (1 lb 9 oz/4 cups) broad beans in the pod, shelled to give 250 g (9 oz)
smoked chicken	1 small
fennel	1 bulb (or 2 baby fennel bulbs)
red capsicum (pepper)	½ small, julienned
salad greens	1 large handful

To make the pistachio pesto, put the basil, rocket, parmesan, garlic and pistachios in a small food processor and process until smooth. Add the oil and process until combined. You will only need half the pesto — store the remainder for a later use. Put half the pesto into a bowl and stir in the cream. Gradually stir in about 1 tablespoon warm water to give a coating consistency. Season with salt and freshly ground black pepper, to taste.

Bring a medium saucepan of water to the boil. Add a large pinch of salt and the broad beans and simmer for 2 minutes. Drain and plunge into iced water. Drain again and peel the skins off the beans, discarding the skins.

Remove the flesh from the chicken and cut it into bite-sized pieces. Very finely slice the fennel lengthways. This is best done using a mandolin. Put the broad beans, chicken, fennel, red capsicum and salad greens in a bowl. Add the pesto and toss well to coat. Serve at once.

To shell the beans, break open the pods and remove the beans

Peel the skin away from the beans and discard the skin

Using a mandolin or sharp knife, slice the fennel very thinly

green pea and smoked ham chowder . . . . serves 4

THIS MAIN-MEAL SOUP IS FILLING AND WHOLESOME, YET LIGHT ENOUGH TO BE SERVED ON THOSE EARLY SPRING DAYS WHEN THE WEATHER IS WARMING AND PEAS ARE AT THEIR SWEETEST. HAM HOCKS CAN BE SALTY; REMOVE EXCESS SALT BY SOAKING THE HOCK IN COLD WATER OVERNIGHT BEFORE MAKING THE SOUP.

carrots	2
oil	2 tablespoons
leek	1, white part only, sliced
onions	2, diced
garlic	2 cloves
celery	1 stalk, diced
smoked ham hock	1
bay leaf	1
thyme	2 sprigs
black peppercorns	1 teaspoon
shelled peas	300 g (10½ oz/2 cups)
mint	3 sprigs, plus 1 small handful leaves
crusty bread	to serve

Cut 1 carrot in half lengthways. Dice the other carrot. Heat the oil in a large heavy-based saucepan and add all of the carrot, the leek, onion, garlic and celery. Cover and cook over low heat for 10 minutes. Add the ham hock, bay leaf, thyme sprigs, peppercorns and 2 litres (70 fl oz/8 cups) water. Slowly bring to the boil, then reduce the heat, cover and simmer for 1 hour, stirring occasionally.

Add half the peas and the mint sprigs to the pan and cook for a further 1 hour, or until the ham falls off the bones. Remove the bones, pull off any meat still attached and return this to the pan. Remove and discard the carrot halves. Add the remaining peas and cook, uncovered, for 5 minutes, or until the peas are tender.

Discard the bay leaf, thyme and mint sprigs. Check the seasoning. Stir through the mint leaves and remove the soup from the heat. Set aside, partially covered, for 3–4 minutes before serving. Serve with crusty bread.

Add the ham hock, bay leaf and thyme sprigs to the pan

Break the meat into bite-sized pieces and return it to the pan

three ways with snow peas

THE ONLY GOOD SNOW PEA IS A FRESH SNOW PEA, SO THIS IS ONE VEGETABLE THAT REALLY DOES NEED TO BE EATEN IN SEASON. TO BRING OUT THEIR NATURAL SWEETNESS AND RETAIN THAT SATISFYING BITE, COOK AS BRIEFLY AS POSSIBLE. THROW THEM INTO A STIR-FRY AT THE LAST MOMENT FOR A TRUE TASTE OF SPRING. THEY ARE ALSO PERFECT FOR TEMPURA; THE FLASH-FRYING CRISPS THE BATTER, HEIGHTENS THE FLAVOUR AND HANGS ONTO THE CRUNCH. OR STEAM THEM BRIEFLY THEN PAIR WITH A TANGY BLOOD ORANGE MAYONNAISE.

stir-fry of snow peas, soy beans, prawns and noodles

Combine 80 ml (2$\frac{1}{2}$ fl oz/$\frac{1}{3}$ cup) each of red wine vinegar and kecap manis, 2 tablespoons each of soy sauce, roasted sesame oil and grated fresh ginger, 1 tablespoon sweet chilli sauce and 1 crushed garlic clove. Cook 250 g (9 oz) dried instant egg noodles in boiling water for 2 minutes, then drain. Peel and devein 140 g (5 oz) raw medium prawns (shrimp), leaving some with their tails on, if desired. Heat 1 tablespoon oil in a large wok over high heat and add the prawns, 200 g (7 oz) small snow peas (mangetout), 1 thinly sliced red capsicum (pepper), 80 g (2$\frac{3}{4}$ oz/$\frac{1}{2}$ cup) thawed frozen soy beans and 6 sliced spring onions (scallions). Stir-fry for 1 minute, or until the prawns are just opaque. Add the noodles and cook for 20–30 seconds. Add the dressing and 2 large handfuls coriander (cilantro) leaves and mix through. Serve immediately. Serves 4.

tempura snow peas

Put 1 egg in a bowl and use chopsticks to lightly break it up. Add 100 g (3$\frac{1}{2}$ oz/$\frac{3}{4}$ cup) plain (all-purpose) flour, 185 ml (6 fl oz/$\frac{3}{4}$ cup) iced water, $\frac{1}{2}$ teaspoon salt and freshly ground black pepper and stir with the chopsticks to combine. Fill a deep-fryer, wok or heavy-based saucepan one-third full of oil and heat to 180°C (350°F), or when a cube of bread dropped into the oil browns in 15 seconds. Lightly coat 150 g (5$\frac{1}{2}$ oz) young snow peas (mangetout) in plain (all-purpose) flour. Working in batches, hold the snow peas by their tails and dip them into the batter. Shake off the excess and carefully drop the snow peas into the hot oil. Cook for 45–60 seconds, or until golden. Drain on paper towels. Serve hot, accompanied by small bowls of ponzu soy sauce, pickled ginger and wasabi paste. Serves 4.

steamed snow peas with blood orange mayonnaise

Whisk together 1 egg yolk, 1 teaspoon white wine vinegar and $\frac{1}{2}$ teaspoon dijon mustard. Whisking constantly, gradually drizzle in 125 ml (4 fl oz/$\frac{1}{2}$ cup) olive oil until you have a thick emulsion. Mix through 1–2 tablespoons fresh blood orange juice, to taste (if unavailable, use fresh orange juice). Season with salt and pepper, to taste. Top and tail 150 g (5$\frac{1}{2}$ oz) snow peas (mangetout) and put them in a steamer. Add 3–4 very thin strips of fresh ginger. Cover and steam over a rolling boil until tender (2–5 minutes, depending on the size and age of the snow peas). Combine the snow peas with $\frac{1}{2}$ sliced celery stalk, 4 spring onions (scallions) that have been sliced on the diagonal and the segments of 1 navel orange. Serve with the mayonnaise. Serves 4.

wax beans with sun-dried tomatoes and capers........................ serves 4

CRISP AND FIRM WITH PLUMP, BLOND BODIES, YELLOW WAX OR BUTTER BEANS HAVE A DELICATE TASTE THAT MAKES THEM A GOOD ACCOMPANIMENT TO SIMPLE DISHES. LIKE ALL FRESH BEANS, THEY LOSE FLAVOUR AND NUTRIENTS ONCE CUT, SO LOOK OUT FOR THE SMALLER ONES THAT CAN BE SERVED WHOLE.

sun-dried tomatoes in oil	2, drained, plus 1 teaspoon of the oil
capers	2 teaspoons, rinsed and drained
young wax beans	250 g (9 oz), tailed
light olive oil	1 teaspoon
lemon	zest of 1, cut into thin strips

Slice the sun-dried tomatoes into long, thin strips. Heat the oil from the sun-dried tomatoes in a small frying pan over medium heat and fry the capers, stirring often, for about 1 minute, until darkened and crisp. Drain on paper towels.

Bring a saucepan of water to the boil. Add a large pinch of salt and the wax beans and simmer for 3–4 minutes, or until just tender. Drain, season with freshly ground black pepper and toss with the sun-dried tomatoes, capers, olive oil and lemon zest. Serve hot or at room temperature.

Wax beans, also known as yellow beans, are like a soft, golden version of string or French beans with a lighter, sweeter taste. Commonly used in Creole cooking, wax beans can replace almost any other variety of fresh bean. Choose fresh, brightly coloured pods that actually snap when bent in half and avoid any that are spotted, leathery or discoloured. Due to selective breeding, most beans no longer need to be stringed before cooking, but if they do, simply snap off the tip and peel away the fibrous string that runs the length of the bean. It is best to cook beans whole; cut beans leach out nutrients during cooking. Store fresh beans in an airtight container in the refrigerator for up to 4 days.

broad bean rotollo with salad greens .... serves 4

YOUNG BROAD (FAVA) BEANS HAVE TENDER PODS THAT CAN BE EATEN LIKE SNOW PEAS (MANGETOUT). AS THEY MATURE, THE PODS BECOME TOUGH, AND THE BEANS MUST BE SHELLED. AS THE PLANT AGES FURTHER, THE SKIN AROUND THE BEANS BECOMES BITTER AND MUST BE REMOVED TO GET TO THE CREAMY FLESH INSIDE.

rotollo

broad (fava) beans	750 g (1 lb 10 oz), shelled to give 275 g (9¾ oz/1½ cups)
eggs	4
egg yolks	4
mint	2 teaspoons finely chopped
basil	2 teaspoons finely chopped
butter	20 g (¾ oz)
pecorino cheese	80 g (2¾ oz) grated

salad

pine nuts	1½ tablespoons
basil	1 tablespoon chopped
olive oil	80 ml (2½ fl oz/⅓ cup)
lemon juice	2 tablespoons
baby cos (romaine) lettuces	2, trimmed
witlof (chicory/Belgian endive), preferably purple	2, trimmed

To make the rotollo, bring a medium saucepan of water to the boil. Add a large pinch of salt and the broad beans and simmer for 2 minutes. Drain and plunge into iced water. Drain and peel the skins off the beans, discarding the skins.

Preheat the oven to 160°C (315°F/Gas 2–3). Beat the eggs, egg yolks, mint and basil together and season with salt and freshly ground black pepper. Melt half the butter in a 20 cm (8 inch) non-stick frying or crepe pan over medium–high heat. Pour in half the egg mixture and cook until the base has set but the top is still a little runny.

Slide the omelette from the pan onto a sheet of baking paper. Scatter half the pecorino and half the broad beans over the surface. Using the baking paper as a guide, gently roll the omelette into a tight sausage. Roll the baking paper around the omelette and tie both ends with string to prevent it from unrolling. Place on a baking sheet. Make another roll with the remaining ingredients and put on the baking sheet. Bake for 8 minutes. Remove from the oven, set aside for 2–3 minutes, then unwrap and set aside to cool.

Put the pine nuts in a small dry saucepan over medium heat and toast, stirring and tossing constantly, for 4–5 minutes, or until the nuts are golden-brown and fragrant. Tip the nuts into a bowl so they do not cook further from the residual heat, and allow to cool.

To make the salad, put 1 tablespoon of the pine nuts, the basil, olive oil and lemon juice in a small food processor or blender and process until smooth. Season with salt and freshly ground black pepper. Put the cos and witlof leaves in a bowl and dress with 2 tablespoons of the dressing.

Slice the rotollo into rounds and scatter over the salad, along with the remaining pine nuts. Drizzle the remaining dressing over the top and serve.

Roll up the filled omelette, using the baking paper to help you

Roll the baking paper around the omelette and tie with string

artichokes

The globe artichoke is a member of the thistle family and the parts that we eat are the immature flower head, the heart and the tender stem immediately below. Artichokes oxidize when their cut surfaces are exposed to air or aluminium. This causes browning and a metallic taste, but these effects can be minimized with a few simple steps.

Prepare a bowl of acidulated water by squeezing the juice from 1 lemon into a large non-aluminium bowl of cold water. If the artichokes have spiky tops to their leaves, snip these off with scissors. Snap off the tough outer leaves until you reach the paler, tender ones. With a stainless steel paring knife, trim around the base, peel the stem and trim the stem to 4–5 cm (1½–2 inches). Rub the cut surfaces with half a lemon. Cut away the top one-third of the globe. As the artichokes are completed, drop them into the acidulated water and put a plate on top to keep them submerged. Let stand for 10 minutes. If the artichokes are to be served halved or quartered, slice them now. Cut away the hairy choke with the point of a knife. If you are serving the artichokes whole, open the leaves from the centre top and dig out the choke with a teaspoon.

Add 1 teaspoon salt and 1 tablespoon each of olive oil and lemon juice to a saucepan of boiling water. Add the artichokes and put a plate on top to keep them submerged. Simmer, uncovered, until a leaf pulls out easily from the base, 15–18 minutes if the artichokes have been quartered, 20–25 minutes if halved, or 30–40 minutes if left whole. Drain whole artichokes by standing them upside down with the stem in the air.

artichoke risotto .... serves 4

THIS RECIPE REQUIRES TENDER YOUNG ARTICHOKES, SO LOOK FOR SMALL GLOBES WITH TIGHTLY OVERLAPPING LEAVES ATOP THICK, STRONG STALKS — AN INDICATION THAT THE GLOBE IS IMMATURE. THE COLOUR OF THE LEAVES VARIES FROM BRILLIANT GREEN, BLUE-GREEN TO VIOLET, ACCORDING TO THE VARIETY OF ARTICHOKE.

lemon	juice of 1
olive oil	2 tablespoons
young globe artichokes	8 small
home-made light chicken or vegetable stock	1.25 litres (44 fl oz/5 cups) (see note)
butter	85 g (3 oz/^{1}/$_3$ cup)
leeks	2, white part only, thinly sliced
arborio rice	325 g (11^1/$_2$ oz/1^1/$_2$ cups)
dry vermouth	125 ml (4 fl oz/^{1}/$_2$ cup)
mint	3 tablespoons chopped
parmesan cheese	50 g (1^3/$_4$ oz/^{1}/$_2$ cup) grated
garlic chives	2 tablespoons chopped (optional)

Prepare the acidulated water and the artichokes according to the method on page 47, up to the cooking stage. Add half the olive oil to the water also and cut the artichoke quarters into thin vertical slices, then return them to the acidulated water.

Heat the stock in a saucepan, cover and keep at a low simmer. Heat the remaining oil and 30 g (1 oz) of the butter over low heat in a large heavy-based non-aluminium pan that is wider than it is tall. Fry the leek without browning for 3–4 minutes. Drain the artichokes and add them to the pan. Cook, stirring, for 1 minute.

Add 250 ml (9 fl oz/1 cup) of stock to the pan, cover and simmer gently for 10 minutes, or until almost all the stock has evaporated. Stir in the rice and cook for 1 minute. Pour in the vermouth and cook until it has been absorbed. Add a ladleful of hot stock and stir constantly over medium heat until all the liquid is absorbed. Continue adding more liquid, a ladleful at a time, until almost all the liquid is absorbed and the rice is tender and creamy. This will take 20–25 minutes. If the stock runs out, use boiling water.

Remove the pan from the heat. Add the remaining butter, the mint and parmesan and stir until the butter has melted. Set aside for 1 minute before serving, topped with the garlic chives, if liked.

Note: The stock needs to be light in colour, as well as flavour.

Slice the artichokes thinly then put them in the acidulated water

Stir the rice in once the first 250 ml of stock has evaporated

bok choy with shiitake mushrooms and sesame

.... serves 4 as an accompaniment

MANY ASIAN GREENS ARE INTERCHANGEABLE AS FAR AS TASTE GOES, AND IT IS THEIR APPEARANCE AND FRESHNESS THAT DETERMINE THE ONES TO USE. BOK CHOY (PAK CHOY) IS READILY AVAILABLE, BUT ONG CHOY (WATER SPINACH) OR ENN CHOY ALSO WORK WELL.

peanut oil	2 tablespoons
garlic	2 cloves, thinly sliced
shiitake mushrooms	100 g (3½ oz), sliced
bok choy (pak choy)	550 g (1 lb 4 oz/1 bunch), trimmed and halved lengthways
sesame oil	1 teaspoon
light soy sauce	1 tablespoon
oyster sauce	1½ tablespoons
sesame seeds	1 teaspoon, roasted

Heat the oil in a large wok over medium–high heat. Fry the garlic for 30–40 seconds, or until crisp and golden. Remove from the wok. Add the mushrooms to the wok and stir-fry for 1–2 minutes, or until browned. Remove from the wok.

Add the bok choy to the wok and stir-fry for 2–3 minutes. Add the sesame oil, soy sauce, oyster sauce and sesame seeds, and return the garlic and mushrooms to the wok. Toss to combine and serve at once.

With their slippery texture and delicate yet earthy flavour, shiitake mushrooms suit a multitude of Asian dishes. While they are more widely available than in the past, you may still need to seek them out. It's worth going to a little trouble; because shiitakes are so distinctive, the more common varieties are not an adequate substitute. Fungi are fragile foodstuffs and really should be eaten on the day they are picked. In the real world, the best you can do is eat them within 1–2 days of purchase. All mushrooms should be stored in the refrigerator in a paper bag (plastic will make them sweat). Shiitakes are also available dried; reconstitute them in warm water for 30 minutes, then cut off the stalk and chop the caps.

summer

Summer bursts into life in a riot of colour and turns the everyday experience of eating into a passionate treat for the senses. The blazing sun intensifies the impact of colour and aroma, heightening sensations yet curbing appetite. The best summer food is swift and simple; effortless meals of wonderful fresh ingredients can be tossed together in no time and spread along the table for all to share. There is no better time of year to nourish yourself, in both body and soul, with crisp, light, vibrant vegetables.

Long sultry days, when the sun is all-encompassing and time seems liquid, are the essence of summer and the perfect backdrop for entertaining at home. This is the time of year when the party season really swings into gear. We're all caterers come the summer months, busy hosting everything from lunch by the pool to a crowd for late-night drinks. Luckily for those palates jaded from the social treadmill, this is the easiest time of year to create a spectacular array of fresh delicacies. That dazzling sunshine has worked its magic in the fields and the summer harvest is a cornucopia of fresh delights.

Salad is the quintessential summer dish and salad vegetables flourish during the warmer months. Tomatoes are at their reddest and ripest; ears of corn hang heavy on the stalk; capsicum, cucumber and lettuce are crisp and fresh. Eating seasonally through the summer months is easy and appealing. The beauty of summer vegetables lies in the intensity of their colour and flavour — it's as though basking in the hot sunshine has imbued them with a special sweetness.

All of this makes them perfect for creating meals that work with the weather. Long, hot days can leave you feeling languid and the idea of a big, hot meal is just too daunting. The key to creating a meal that is light and yet still satisfying is to go small on quantity but big on flavour. The perfect summer dish is one that fills you up without weighing you down. Seafood and lean meats served with piles of delectable vegetables and salads work brilliantly whether you're hosting a party by the pool or just sitting down to a quiet dinner at home.

As with all cooking, the key to getting the most out of summer vegetables lies in technique. Quick and easy are the catchwords for summer eating. When the mercury is rising, there is little appeal in stoking up the oven in an already hot house. So fire up the barbie, try a little flash-frying or just revel in the natural sweetness in a pile of fresh vegetables. Summer is finally here and it's time to celebrate this season of plenty.

eggplant, mozzarella and red capsicum stack

MOZZARELLA IS A FRESH, SPRINGY CHEESE TRADITIONALLY MADE WITH BUFFALO'S MILK, ALTHOUGH COW'S MILK IS NOW OFTEN USED. MOZZARELLA HAS AN ELASTICITY THAT MAKES IT EXCELLENT FOR MELTING, AS IN THIS RECIPE. BUY THE MOZZARELLA FIRST, THEN CHOOSE EGGPLANT OF ROUGHLY THE SAME DIAMETER.

eggplants (aubergines)	2 small (about 280 g/10 oz each)
red capsicums (peppers)	2 small, halved and seeded
olive oil	125 ml (4 fl oz/1/2 cup)
seasoned plain (all-purpose) flour	for dusting
mozzarella (preferably buffalo)	250 g (9 oz)
provolone cheese	70 g (21/2 oz/1/2 cup) finely grated
thyme	2 teaspoons
basil	1 tablespoon shredded

Cut each eggplant into six 1.5 cm (5/8 inch) thick rounds, put the slices in a colander and sprinkle with salt. Set aside for 30 minutes. Rinse and dry well with paper towels.

Cook the capsicums, skin side up, under a hot grill (broiler) until the skins blacken and blister. Cool in a plastic bag, then peel. Cut each capsicum half into 2 pieces roughly the same shape as the eggplant slices.

Heat half the olive oil in a large frying pan until medium–hot. Lightly dust the eggplant slices with the seasoned flour and fry in batches for about 6 minutes, until golden on both sides but still firm, adding more oil as required. Drain on paper towels.

Preheat the oven to 190°C (375°F/Gas 5). Cut the mozzarella into twelve 1 cm (1/2 inch) slices. Grease a small baking dish, about 16 cm (61/4 inches) square and 6 cm (21/2 inches) deep. Arrange 4 slices of eggplant in the dish and top each slice with a slice of mozzarella, a sprinkling of provolone and a piece of red capsicum. Scatter with some thyme and basil. Repeat this layering once more. Finish with the last of the eggplant, then the mozzarella. Scatter the remaining provolone over the top.

Stick a wooden skewer or toothpick through the centre of each stack to keep the layers in place. Bake for 35 minutes, or until the mozzarella has melted and the top is golden brown. Transfer the stacks to 4 serving plates, remove the skewers and serve hot, before the mozzarella cools and becomes rubbery.

Slice each roasted capsicum half into two pieces

Layer the eggplant, mozzarella, provolone and capsicum

sweet potato, zucchini and smoked trout frittata . . . . serves 4

THE SKINS OF SWEET POTATOES MAY BE ORANGE, PURPLE OR CREAM AND THE FLESH WHITE, APRICOT OR ORANGE, WITH THE TEXTURE BECOMING DRIER AS THE COLOUR DEEPENS. FOR THIS RECIPE, USE WHICHEVER TYPE YOU PREFER, OR WHATEVER IS AVAILABLE.

sweet potato	250 g (9 oz) diced
vegetable oil	2 teaspoons
butter	20 g (³/4 oz)
brown onion	1, halved, thinly sliced
garlic	1 clove, crushed
zucchini (courgettes)	2 medium, cut into 5 mm (¹/4 inch) slices
smoked trout fillet	500 g (1 lb 2 oz), broken into bite-sized pieces
eggs	8, lightly beaten
dill	2 teaspoons chopped

Blanch the sweet potato in boiling salted water for 5 minutes. Drain and set aside.

Heat the oil and butter in a 25 cm (10 inch) non-stick frying pan and swirl it around to coat the sides of the pan. Add the onion and fry without browning over medium–low heat for 5 minutes. Add the garlic and zucchini slices, increase the heat to medium and fry until golden, 4–5 minutes. Add the smoked trout and pour the eggs in. Stir gently to mix through. Scatter the reserved sweet potato and dill over the top.

Preheat the grill (broiler) to high.

Cover the frying pan and cook until the bottom of the eggs sets, about 5 minutes. Check once or twice and reduce the heat if you feel that the bottom might be burning. Loosen the mixture around the edges and shake the pan to dislodge the frittata.

Wrap a dry cloth around the handle of the pan and position the pan 10–12 cm (4–4¹/2 inches) under the grill. Cook until lightly golden and set, 1–2 minutes. Slide the frittata onto a plate and slice into quarters. Serve with a green salad.

Pour the beaten eggs over the smoked trout and vegetables

Scatter the sweet potato and dill over the top of the frittata

pappardelle with zucchini flowers and goat's cheese

serves 4

ZUCCHINI (COURGETTE) FLOWERS, WHICH ARE EDIBLE, DO NOT LAST LONG ONCE PICKED AND ARE A FLEETING DELIGHT OF SUMMER. THEY ARE USUALLY STUFFED, THEN BAKED OR FRIED. BEFORE USING, REMOVE AND DISCARD THE STAMEN FROM INSIDE THE FLOWER, WASH THE FLOWER AND MAKE SURE IT DOES NOT HARBOUR ANY INSECTS.

ricotta cheese	175 g (6 oz/³/₄ cup)
thick (double/heavy) cream	125 ml (4 fl oz/¹/₂ cup)
thyme	2 teaspoons
ground nutmeg	¹/₄ teaspoon
dried pappardelle	300 g (10¹/₂ oz) (or 400 g (14 oz) fresh pappardelle or other ribbon pasta)
olive oil	60 ml (2 fl oz/¹/₄ cup)
zucchini (courgettes)	4 small, cut into thin batons
zucchini (courgette) flowers	16, no vegetable attached
plain (all-purpose) flour	for dusting
soft goat's cheese	100 g (3¹/₂ oz)

Combine the ricotta, cream, thyme and nutmeg in a bowl and season well with salt and white pepper. Set aside in a cool place (do not refrigerate) for 1 hour.

Cook the pasta in a saucepan of boiling salted water until *al dente* according to the manufacturer's instructions.

Meanwhile, heat the olive oil in a large frying pan over medium–high heat and cook the zucchini for 4 minutes, or until lightly golden. Remove the zucchini with a slotted spoon and drain on paper towels. Dust the zucchini flowers with flour, shake off the excess and fry for about 1 minute, until lightly golden.

Drain the pasta and transfer to a large serving dish. Add the zucchini, zucchini flowers and ricotta mixture and toss lightly. Dot with small pieces of goat's cheese and serve immediately.

The most ethereal of summer delicacies, zucchini (courgette) flowers somehow slipped off the list of edibles before being rediscovered via Italian restaurants. Rampant throughout the summer months, zucchini flowers are like nature's gift to stuffed cuisine and one of the most delicious ways to eat cheese. As their popularity increases, they have become easier to source, but if you can't find them at the supermarket, ask your local grocer. Male flowers have a stalk; the female ones have baby zucchini attached. Both are edible. Like all flowers, those from the zucchini vine only last a few days after being picked, so make sure you buy them on the day you plan to use them.

okra curry with chicken .... serves 4

OKRA FEATURES IN THE COOKING OF MANY AFRICAN, ASIAN AND CARIBBEAN COUNTRIES, WHERE IT IS VALUED FOR ITS FLAVOUR AS WELL AS FOR THE MUCILAGE IT CONTAINS. THIS GLUEY LIQUID IS RELEASED WHEN THE FLESH IS CUT, AND ACTS AS A THICKENING AGENT IN STEWS AND SOUPS.

chilli flakes	1 teaspoon
turmeric	1/2 teaspoon
cumin seeds	1/2 teaspoon
white peppercorns	4
desiccated coconut	30 g (1 oz/1/3 cup)
okra	500 g (1 lb 2 oz)
oil	2 tablespoons
onions	2, sliced lengthways
garlic	3 cloves, crushed
chicken thigh fillets	400 g (14 oz), trimmed and cut into quarters
tomato	1 large, chopped
sugar	1 teaspoon
coconut milk	250 ml (9 fl oz/1 cup)
chicken stock	375 ml (13 fl oz/1 1/2 cups)
malt vinegar	1 tablespoon
boiled rice or flat bread	to serve

Grind the chilli flakes, turmeric, cumin, peppercorns and coconut in a spice mill or with a mortar and pestle until uniform.

Trim the okra by cutting off the tip and the tough stem end, being careful not to cut into the body.

Heat the oil in a deep frying pan over medium heat. Fry the onion and garlic for about 5 minutes, or until light brown. Stir in the spice mixture and fry for 1 minute. Add the okra, chicken, tomato, sugar, coconut milk and chicken stock and bring to the boil.

Reduce the heat and simmer gently for 20 minutes. Add the vinegar and 1 teaspoon salt and simmer for 5 minutes. Check the seasoning. Serve with boiled rice or a flat bread such as puri or chapatti.

Okra, sometimes known as ladies' fingers, has been long neglected as a vegetable in the West. It can be used raw or blanched in salads, or cooked in a variety of ways. It is wonderful in casseroles or stews, as long, slow cooking renders it soft and full of flavour. Okra should be eaten young, when the pods are still crisp and palatable. Buy pods that are tender and bright green in colour. They should be no longer than 6 cm (2 1/2 inches), and should snap rather than bend. If too ripe, the pods will feel sticky. If using as a thickener, add the sliced pods about 10 minutes before the end of cooking. In some recipes, the pod is used whole, thus preventing the release of the sticky substances within.

tunisian eggplant salad with preserved lemon

serves 4

EGGPLANT (AUBERGINE) IS COMMON IN TUNISIAN SALADS AND STEWS. THE CUBED FLESH MAY BE SALTED FOR UP TO 24 HOURS TO EXTRACT ALL THE MOISTURE, SO THAT VERY LITTLE OIL IS REQUIRED FOR FRYING. THIS SALAD IS BEST MADE IN ADVANCE AND LEFT FOR SEVERAL HOURS FOR THE FLAVOURS TO MERGE.

eggplants (aubergines)	2 large
olive oil	125 ml (4 fl oz/½ cup)
cumin seeds	1 teaspoon
garlic	2 cloves, very thinly sliced
currants	1 tablespoon
slivered almonds	1 tablespoon
roma (plum) tomatoes	6 small, quartered lengthways
dried oregano	1 teaspoon
red bird's eye chillies	4, halved lengthways and seeded
lemon juice	2 tablespoons
parsley	4 tablespoons chopped
preserved or salted lemon	½
extra virgin olive oil	to serve

Cut the eggplants into 2 cm (³⁄₄ inch) cubes, put in a large colander and sprinkle with 1–2 teaspoons salt. Set aside to drain in the sink for 2–3 hours. Dry with paper towels.

Heat half the olive oil in a large flameproof casserole dish over medium–high heat. Fry the eggplant in batches for 5–6 minutes, or until golden, adding more oil as required. Drain on crumpled paper towels.

Reduce the heat and add any remaining oil to the casserole dish, along with the cumin, garlic, currants and almonds. Fry for 20–30 seconds, or until the garlic starts to colour. Add the tomato and oregano and cook for 1 minute. Remove from the heat.

Trim the rind from the piece of preserved lemon and cut the rind into thin strips. Discard the flesh.

Return the eggplant to the casserole and add the chilli, lemon juice, parsley and preserved lemon rind. Toss gently and season with freshly ground black pepper. Set aside at room temperature for at least 1 hour before serving. Check the seasoning, then drizzle with extra virgin olive oil.

Add the tomato and oregano to the pan and fry for 1 minute

Slice the rind of the preserved lemon into thin strips

three ways with zucchini

ZUCCHINI IS A WONDROUS VEGETABLE — UBIQUITOUS TO THE POINT OF BEING COMMONPLACE, BUT ALSO EXTREMELY VERSATILE. ZUCCHINI RESPONDS JUST AS WELL TO A LONG SLOW BRAISE AS IT DOES A QUICK TOSS IN THE FRYING PAN. IT CAN ALSO BE EATEN RAW, AND IS ONE OF THE FEW VEGETABLES THAT ACTUALLY GOES WELL IN SWEET DISHES. TRY IT IN A CRISP SALAD WITH SHARP FETA AND FIERY RADISH. GO FOR SOMETHING UNUSUAL WITH A ZUCCHINI SOUFFLÉ OR DRAW OUT ITS DELICATE FLAVOUR IN FRAGRANT, HERBY SOUP.

fragrant zucchini, coconut and green pea soup

Heat 1½ tablespoons oil in a large saucepan over low heat. Gently fry the sliced white part of 1 large leek for 5 minutes. Add 1 teaspoon grated fresh ginger and 2 crushed garlic cloves and fry for 1 minute. Stir in 425 g (15 oz) diced zucchini (courgette), 125 g (4½ oz/¾ cup) shelled peas, 1 tablespoon each of torn basil and mint and 750 ml (26 fl oz/3 cups) water. Simmer for 15 minutes. Transfer to a blender or food processor and blend until smooth. Return to the pan with 250 ml (9 fl oz/1 cup) light chicken stock and 250 ml (9 fl oz/1 cup) coconut cream and bring to the boil. Cut 425 g (15 oz) zucchini into 2 cm (¾ inch) cubes and add to the pan. Simmer for 6–8 minutes, or until just tender. Check the seasoning and stir in 1 tablespoon each of young basil leaves and small mint leaves. Set aside for 4–5 minutes before serving warm. Serves 4.

zucchini, radish and feta salad

To make the dressing, combine 1 tablespoon white wine vinegar, 2 tablespoons olive oil, 2–3 teaspoons wholegrain mustard and salt and freshly ground black pepper, to taste. Finely shave 5 small zucchini (courgettes) from top to bottom. Place in a colander, sprinkle with 2 teaspoons salt and set aside to drain in the sink for 30 minutes. Do not rinse. Gently dry with paper towels and put in a large bowl. Finely slice 6 radishes and ½ small red onion lengthways and add to the bowl. Tear the inner leaves of 1 small cos (romaine) lettuce into smaller pieces and add to the bowl. Add the dressing and toss lightly. Transfer to a shallow serving dish and crumble 100 g (3½ oz/⅔ cup) feta cheese over the top before serving. Serves 4.

zucchini soufflé

Butter four 125 ml (4 fl oz/½ cup) soufflé dishes and coat with finely grated parmesan cheese, about 1 tablespoon in total. Wrap a double sheet of baking paper around each dish, protruding 5 cm (2 inches) above the rim. Secure in place with string. Steam 350 g (12 oz) zucchini (courgettes) until just tender. Blend in a food processor with 125 ml (4 fl oz/½ cup) evaporated milk until smooth. Melt 30 g (1 oz) butter in a saucepan over low heat and stir in 2 tablespoons plain (all-purpose) flour. Cook, stirring, for 2–3 minutes. Stir in the zucchini mixture and cook for 3 minutes. Transfer to a bowl and stir through 1 tablespoon chopped basil, 80 g (2¾ oz/⅔ cups) grated emmental cheese, 4 egg yolks and a pinch of ground nutmeg. Season with salt and pepper. In a separate bowl, whisk 4 egg whites until soft peaks form. Fold one-quarter of the egg white through the zucchini mixture, then lightly fold in the rest. Spoon into the prepared dishes, place on a baking sheet and bake in a preheated 180°C (350°F/Gas 4) oven for 40–45 minutes, or until risen and golden. Serve immediately. Serves 4.

fragrant zucchini, coconut and green pea soup

tomato, red capsicum and saffron tart

serves 4–6

TOMATOES AND CAPSICUMS (PEPPERS) ARE AT THEIR MOST FLAVOURSOME AND ABUNDANT IN LATE SUMMER. TAKE ADVANTAGE OF THEIR BOUNTY IN A SAFFRON-INFUSED TART, A SLICE OF WHICH IS LIKE A LATE-SUMMER SKYLINE AFTER A PERFECT DAY: VIBRANT, COLOURFUL AND HAPPY.

pastry

plain (all-purpose) flour	250 g (9 oz/2 cups)
butter	125 g (4¹/₂ oz), chilled and diced
chilled water	3–4 tablespoons

filling

roma (plum) tomatoes	600 g (1 lb 5 oz), peeled, seeded and cored
red capsicum (pepper)	1 large, halved and seeded
olive oil	1 tablespoon
onion	1 small, finely chopped
garlic	2 cloves, crushed
oregano	1 sprig
tomato paste (concentrated purée)	1 tablespoon
bay leaf	1
dark muscovado sugar	1 teaspoon
dry white wine	80 ml (2¹/₂ fl oz/¹/₃ cup)
chicken stock	125 ml (4 fl oz/¹/₂ cup)

custard

saffron threads	1 scant teaspoon
cream (whipping)	350 ml (12 fl oz)
eggs	2
egg yolks	4

To make the pastry, put the flour and butter in a food processor with a large pinch of salt. Process in short bursts, using the pulse button, until the mixture is fine and crumbly. Add most of the water and again, process in short bursts until the mixture just comes together in small balls. Turn the mixture out onto a lightly floured surface and press together to form a clump. Cover with plastic wrap and chill for 30 minutes.

Coarsely chop the flesh of the tomatoes. Finely chop half the red capsicum. Heat the olive oil in a large frying pan over low heat. Fry the onion, garlic and oregano for 5 minutes. Stir in the tomato, chopped capsicum, tomato paste, bay leaf, sugar and wine and cook for 15 minutes. Add the stock and simmer for 15 minutes, or until the sauce is thick and all the liquid has evaporated.

To make the custard, soak the saffron in 1 tablespoon hot water for 15 minutes. Put the saffron and water in a small saucepan with the cream and slowly heat to body temperature. Turn off the heat. Beat the eggs and yolks together in a bowl. Add the saffron cream and mix well. Season with salt and pepper, to taste.

Preheat the oven to 200°C (400°F/Gas 6). Grease a 28 x 20 cm (11 x 8 inch) rectangular tart tin. Roll out the pastry on a lightly floured surface to a rectangle large enough to line the base and sides of the tin. Fit the pastry into the tin, neatening the edges. Line the pastry with crumpled baking paper, fill with baking weights or dried beans and bake blind for 18 minutes. Remove the weights and paper and bake for a further 18 minutes. Set aside to cool for 10 minutes. Reduce the oven temperature to 180°C (350°F/Gas 4) and put a baking sheet on the middle shelf.

Discard the bay leaf and oregano sprig from the filling. Spread the filling over the base of the pastry shell. Gently pour the custard over the top. Cut the remaining red capsicum into 7–8 strips and arrange over the custard in a parallel row from one corner to its diagonal opposite. Put the tart on the baking sheet and bake for 30–40 minutes, or until set and golden.

Simmer the filling until it is thick and the liquid has evaporated

Gently pour the custard over the filling in the tart tin

vietnamese cucumber salad with steamed fish

STEAMING FISH, WHETHER WHOLE OR IN SLICES, IS A COMMON COOKING METHOD IN SOUTHEAST ASIA. A CRISP, REFRESHING SALAD WITH A SOUR-SWEET DRESSING IS A PERFECT COMPLEMENT. LING, MONKFISH AND HAKE ARE SUITABLE SUBSTITUTES FOR THE COD IN THIS RECIPE.

salad

lime juice	1 teaspoon
sweet chilli sauce	2 tablespoons
fish sauce	1–2 tablespoons
palm sugar	1/2–1 tablespoon grated (or raw caster (superfine) sugar)
Lebanese (short) cucumbers	4, cut into 2 cm (3/4 inch) chunks
red onion	1/2, sliced
pear	1 large
Vietnamese mint	1 small handful
Thai basil	1 small handful
lemon grass	2 stems, trimmed, finely chopped
fish sauce	80 ml (2 1/2 fl oz/1/3 cup)
palm sugar	50 g (1 3/4 oz/1/4 cup) grated (or raw caster (superfine) sugar)
cod fillets	1 kg (2 lb 4 oz)
roasted unsalted peanuts	80 g (2 3/4 oz/1/2 cup) chopped

To make the salad, combine the lime juice and sweet chilli sauce in a large bowl and add the fish sauce and palm sugar, to taste. Add the cucumber and onion. Quarter and core the pear, slice it thinly and add it to the bowl. Chop half the mint and basil leaves, add to the bowl and toss to coat. Cover and set aside in a cool place for 2 hours.

Meanwhile, combine the lemon grass, fish sauce and palm sugar in a large bowl. Slice the cod into 1 cm (1/2 inch) thick slices and add to the bowl. Toss to coat, cover with plastic wrap and chill for 1 hour.

Line a large bamboo steamer with baking paper and cover with as many slices of cod as will fit in a single layer. Place over a wok or saucepan of boiling water and steam for 4 minutes, or until cooked through. Repeat with the remaining fish.

To serve, toss the remaining mint leaves and the peanuts through the salad. Divide among 4 serving plates and top with the fish and the remaining basil leaves.

Quarter and core the pear, then slice it thinly

Steam fish in a single layer in a steamer lined with baking paper

three ways with sweet corn

NO VEGETABLE IS MORE EMBLEMATIC OF SUMMER THAN SWEET CORN. THE BRIGHT YELLOW KERNELS AND SWEET JUICE CONJURE MEMORIES OF THE ENDLESS SUMMERS OF CHILDHOOD, AND CORN'S POPULARITY MAKES IT PERFECT FOR SUMMER PARTIES AND BARBECUES. SERVED WARM, SOUFFLE-LIKE CORN SPOONBREAD FROM THE AMERICAN SOUTH MAKES A SATISFYING SIDE DISH. SPICY CORN FRITTERS, FRAGRANT WITH THAI HERBS, ARE GREAT FOR PASSING ROUND ON A PLATTER. OR FIRE UP THE BARBECUE FOR SWEET CORN AND CHICKEN.

corn spoonbread

Combine 250 g (9 oz/1 cup) crème fraîche, 1 egg, 25 g (1 oz/1/4 cup) grated parmesan cheese and 30 g (1 oz/1/4 cup) self-raising flour in a large bowl. Slice the kernels off 3 sweet corn cobs and add to the bowl. Add a pinch of cayenne pepper, and salt and freshly ground black pepper, to taste. Spoon into a greased shallow 18 cm (7 inch) square ovenproof dish. Sprinkle with 2 tablespoons grated parmesan cheese and dot with 40 g (1½ oz) butter. Bake in a preheated 190°C (375°F/Gas 5) oven for 30–35 minutes, or until set and golden brown. Serve immediately, straight from the dish. Serves 4.

thai sweet corn cakes with chilli dipping sauce

To make the dipping sauce, put 1 tablespoon fish sauce, 2 tablespoons cold water, 1/2 teaspoon grated palm sugar, 2 teaspoons rice vinegar, 1 seeded and finely chopped red bird's eye chilli and 1 teaspoon finely chopped coriander (cilantro) stems in a small bowl and whisk until the sugar has dissolved. Slice the kernels off 3 medium sweet corn cobs. You will need 400 g (14 oz/2 cups) in total. Put 200 g (7 oz/1 cup) of the corn in a food processor with 2 chopped garlic cloves, 3 teaspoons grated fresh ginger, 1/2 seeded and chopped large red chilli, 30 g (1 oz/1/4 cup) plain (all-purpose) flour, 1/2 teaspoon grated palm sugar, 2 tablespoons coarsely chopped coriander (cilantro) leaves, 1 teaspoon fish sauce and 2 eggs. Process until the mixture is chopped medium–fine. Transfer to a bowl and stir through the remaining corn kernels. Check the seasoning. Heat 60 ml (2 fl oz/1/4 cup) oil in a large frying pan over medium heat. Spoon heaped tablespoons of the corn mixture into the pan and fry for 1–1½ minutes each side, or until browned. Serve hot with the dipping sauce. Makes 12.

barbecued sweet corn, chicken and tomatoes with opal basil

Strip the husks and silks off 2 small sweet corn cobs, halve 4 roma (plum) tomatoes lengthways and trim a 200 g (7 oz) chicken breast fillet. Brush the chicken and vegetables with 60 ml (2 fl oz/1/4 cup) olive oil. Cook on medium–high heat on a preheated barbecue plate or chargrill pan, 4–5 minutes for the tomatoes and 6–8 minutes for both the corn and the chicken. Transfer the tomatoes to a large bowl. Slice the corn into 2 cm (3/4 inch) rounds, cut the chicken into 1 cm (1/2 inch) slices and add to the tomatoes. Add 1 small handful opal (purple) basil, torn if large. Combine 80 ml (2½ fl oz/1/3 cup) olive oil, 2 tablespoons each of lemon juice and dijon mustard, 1 crushed garlic clove and a pinch of sugar in a small bowl. Season with salt and freshly ground black pepper, to taste. Add 2 tablespoons of the dressing to the chicken mixture and toss gently. Arrange the corn, tomatoes and chicken in a pile on 4 serving plates and drizzle with the remaining dressing. Serves 4.

roasted capsicum, chilli
and semi-dried tomato spread................serves 4

SERVE THIS SPREAD WITH CRUDITES, TOASTED TURKISH BREAD FINGERS OR OTHER BREADS AND CRACKERS. IT ALSO GOES WELL WITH BOILED OR ROASTED NEW POTATOES. STORE THE SPREAD, COVERED, IN THE REFRIGERATOR FOR UP TO 5 DAYS.

red capsicum (pepper)	1 large, quartered and seeded
semi-dried (sun-blushed) tomatoes	90 g (3¼ oz/⅔ cup)
sambal oelek	2 teaspoons
spreadable cream cheese	125 g (4½ oz/½ cup)
basil	2 tablespoons chopped

Preheat the grill (broiler) to high. Arrange the capsicum, skin side up, on the grill rack and grill (broil) for 10 minutes, or until well blackened. Cool in a plastic bag, then peel and discard the skin. Chop the flesh.

Drain the tomatoes well on paper towels, pat dry and roughly chop. Put in a small food processor fitted with the metal blade and add the capsicum, sambal oelek, cream cheese and basil. Whizz for 10 seconds, or until roughly combined. The tomatoes should still have some texture. Season well with salt and freshly ground black pepper.

Peel away and discard the skin from the roasted capsicum

Put all the ingredients in the bowl of a food processor

Process until coarsely chopped but still retaining some texture

thai red squash curry . . . . serves 4

THAI COOKING USES SEVERAL KINDS OF CURRY PASTES, EACH WITH A DISTINCT FLAVOUR AND COLOUR OBTAINED FROM ITS BLEND OF HERBS AND SPICES. RED CURRY PASTE IS HIGHLY FRAGRANT. THE COMMERCIAL BRANDS VARY FROM MEDIUM TO HOT IN INTENSITY, SO ADD MORE OR LESS TO SUIT YOUR TASTE.

oil	2 tablespoons
Thai red curry paste	1–2 tablespoons
coconut milk	400 ml (14 fl oz)
soy sauce	2 tablespoons
light vegetable stock	125 ml (4 fl oz/1/2 cup)
palm sugar	2 teaspoons grated
baby (pattypan) squash	700 g (1 lb 9 oz), halved, or quartered if large
baby corn	100 g (31/2 oz), halved lengthways
snow peas (mangetout)	100 g (31/2 oz), topped and tailed
lime juice	2 teaspoons
unsalted roasted cashews	35 g (11/4 oz/1/3 cup), coarsely chopped
lime wedges	to serve (optional)

Heat the oil in a large saucepan over medium–high heat and fry the curry paste for 1–2 minutes, or until the paste separates. Add the coconut milk, soy sauce, stock and palm sugar and stir until the sugar has melted. Bring to the boil.

Add the squash to the pan and return to the boil. Add the baby corn and simmer, covered, for 12–15 minutes, or until the squash is just tender. Add the snowpeas and lime juice and simmer, uncovered, for 1 minute. Serve with cashews scattered over the top, and accompanied by the lime wedges if desired.

Note: If baby squash are unavailable, use zucchini (courgettes), cut into slices 2.5 cm (1 inch) thick.

Baby (pattypan) squash are among the cutest members of the vegetable kingdom. These brightly coloured buttons of goodness belong to the marrow family, which also includes winter squash (pumpkins), cucumbers, melons, and gourds. Fresh and snappy when eaten raw, they are fabulously soft and luscious once cooked. With their subtle, sunny flavour, they are delicious with a dressing and lend themselves to a wide range of seasonings. Abundant throughout summer, they may be green and/or yellow in colour. Like all summer squash, the skin of baby squash is edible. Both the skin and flesh are firmer than those of other summer squash, however, which makes this squash good for baking and stewing.

eggplant salad with prosciutto . . . . serves 4

PROSCIUTTO IS THE ITALIAN WORD FOR HAM, MORE PARTICULARLY FOR VARIOUS TYPES OF RAW HAM, OR PROSCIUTTO CRUDO. THE BEST KNOWN OF THESE IS PROBABLY THAT FROM AROUND THE TOWN OF PARMA, IN EMILIA-ROMAGNA. PROSCIUTTO IS USUALLY THINLY SLICED AND SERVED AS A STARTER OR, AS HERE, IN A SALAD.

dressing

olive oil	2 tablespoons
hazelnut oil	1 1/2 tablespoons
Spanish sherry vinegar	1 tablespoon
garlic	2 cloves, bruised
eggplants (aubergines)	2 small (300 g/10 1/2 oz each)
olive oil	170 ml (5 1/2 fl oz/2/3 cup)
red coral lettuce	1/2 bunch
opal (purple) basil	1 small handful
yellow cherry tomatoes	250 g (9 oz)
prosciutto	100 g (3 1/2 oz) sliced

To make the dressing, combine the olive oil, hazelnut oil, vinegar and garlic in a small bowl and mix well to combine. Season with salt and freshly ground black pepper, to taste. Set aside for 1 hour to infuse. Discard the garlic cloves.

Slice the eggplant lengthways into 1.5 cm (5/8 inch) slices, discarding the outer slices that have skin on one face. Put in a colander and sprinkle with 2–3 teaspoons salt. Set aside to drain in the sink for 30 minutes. Rinse and dry with paper towels.

Heat half the olive oil in a frying pan over medium heat. Fry the eggplant, in batches, for 7–8 minutes, or until lightly brown but tender, adding more oil as required. Drain on paper towels.

Tear the lettuce into large bite-sized pieces and spread in a shallow serving dish. Add the eggplant slices, basil and whole cherry tomatoes and toss lightly. Clump the prosciutto slices into loose bundles and mix in between the other ingredients. Drizzle with the dressing just before serving.

Put the eggplant slices in a colander and sprinkle with salt

Tear the lettuce into bite-sized pieces

three ways with rocket

LONG A STAPLE OF SOUTHERN EUROPE, WHERE IT GROWS WILD, THIS POWERFUL LITTLE LEAF WAS THE CULINARY REDISCOVERY OF THE 1990S, LEAPING EASILY FROM RESTAURANT PLATE TO THE HOME KITCHEN. WHILE IT ADDS A HOT LITTLE KICK TO SALADS, IT'S ALSO FABULOUS ADDED TO A COOKED DISH. GET OUT THE MORTAR AND PESTLE FOR PESTO WITH A PUNCH, SPICE UP LITTLE TARTS WITH A HANDFUL OF ROCKET, OR MIX THE PEPPERY LEAVES WITH SOME TART BLUE CHEESE AND SALTY PANCETTA FOR A DISH THAT DOESN'T HOLD BACK ON FLAVOUR.

rocket pesto on cheese tortellini

To make the pesto, put 60 g (2^{1}/4 oz/1^{2}/3 cups) baby rocket (arugula), 1 small handful parsley, 2 crushed garlic cloves and 20 g (^{3}/4 oz/^{1}/4 cup) golden walnuts in a food processor and blend until smooth. Add 35 g (1^{1}/4 oz/^{1}/3 cup) finely grated parmesan cheese and mix through. With the motor running, drizzle in 125 ml (4 fl oz/^{1}/2 cup) olive oil in a thin stream. Season with salt and a little freshly ground black pepper. Stir in enough water (1–1^{1}/2 tablespoons) to give a good coating consistency. Cook 1 kg (2 lb 4 oz) cheese tortellini in a saucepan of boiling salted water according to the manufacturer's instructions. Drain and toss with 2–3 tablespoons of the pesto. Divide among 4 bowls, spoon a little more pesto over each serving and top with shavings of parmesan cheese. Serves 4. Store the remaining pesto in a sealed container in the refrigerator for up to 5 days.

rocket tarts

Cut four 15 cm (6 inch) circles from 2 sheets of ready-rolled puff pastry and use them to line 4 greased 10 cm (4 inch) loose-based tartlet tins. Prick the bases with a fork. Line the pastry with crumpled baking paper, fill with baking weights or dried beans and bake blind in a preheated 180°C (350°F/Gas 4) oven for 15 minutes. Remove the weights and paper and bake for a further 5 minutes. Heat 1 tablespoon olive oil in a frying pan over medium heat and gently cook ^{1}/2 finely diced small onion for 5 minutes. Stir in 1 large handful baby rocket (arugula) leaves and remove from the heat. Put 3 beaten eggs, 125 g (4^{1}/2 oz/^{1}/2 cup) ricotta cheese and a pinch of ground nutmeg into a small bowl, with salt and pepper, to taste. Beat lightly, leaving some of the ricotta in lumps. Stir in the rocket mixture. Spoon into the pastry shells and bake for about 25 minutes, until set. Serves 4.

rocket with pancetta and gorgonzola dressing

To make the dressing, mash 50 g (1^{3}/4 oz) Gorgonzola or other blue cheese with ^{1}/2 crushed garlic clove in a small food processor. With the motor running, gradually add 1^{1}/2 tablespoons olive oil, then 3 teaspoons white wine vinegar. Remove from the processor and stir through 60 ml (2 fl oz/^{1}/4 cup) cream and ^{1}/2 teaspoon chopped tarragon. Season with freshly ground black pepper. Grill (broil) 6 thin slices of pancetta under a preheated hot grill (broiler) for 3–4 minutes, or until crisp. Cool, then break into shards. Put 2 large handfuls rocket (arugula) leaves, 2 tablespoons roasted pine nuts, the pancetta and the dressing in a bowl and toss together. Serve immediately. Serves 4.

summer salad of mixed salad greens, mango, avocado and prawns . . . . serves 4

AVOCADOS HAVE SOFT, BUTTERY FLESH, A MILD, SLIGHTLY NUTTY FLAVOUR, AND SKINS THAT MAY BE SMOOTH OR ROUGH. CUT AVOCADO TURNS BROWN, SO CUT IT JUST BEFORE USE OR BRUSH IT WITH LEMON JUICE TO PREVENT DISCOLOURATION. FIRM, UNRIPE AVOCADOS WILL RIPEN AT ROOM TEMPERATURE AFTER 3–4 DAYS.

dressing

olive oil	80 ml (2½ fl oz/⅓ cup)
white wine vinegar	1 tablespoon
dijon mustard	1 tablespoon
orange zest	1 teaspoon grated
raw medium prawns (shrimp)	24 (about 600 g/1 lb 5 oz), peeled and deveined, tails intact
red onion	1 small
avocados	2
mangoes	2
baby cos (romaine) lettuce	1
red oakleaf lettuce	½
butter lettuce	½

To make the dressing, put the olive oil, vinegar, mustard and orange zest in a small bowl and mix well. Season with salt and freshly ground black pepper, to taste.

Preheat a barbecue or chargrill pan to medium heat. Brush the prawns with a little of the dressing, arrange on the grill plate or pan and cook for 5 minutes, or until crisp and opaque. Transfer to a large bowl.

Finely slice the onion lengthways and add to the bowl. Slice the avocados into large wedges and add to the bowl. Slice the cheeks off the mangoes and peel them. Cut into slices and add to the bowl.

Discard the damaged outer leaves of the lettuces and tear the leaves into smaller pieces. Add to the bowl. Pour in the dressing and toss lightly before serving.

Long gone are the days when lettuce meant iceberg and only iceberg. An extensive range of fresh lettuces is now available. Some of the varieties so differ in taste and texture that it seems the name is all that they have in common. Whether soft, leafy, crisp or bitter, any and all of these lettuces make a fabulous salad alone or tossed together. Lettuce is at its best in summer and should be stored either in a lettuce crisper or wrapped in a damp tea-towel in the fridge. Wash thoroughly and dry well, using paper towels, tea towels, or a salad spinner; any moisture left on the leaves will dilute the dressing. A quick soak in cold water can revive slightly limp leaves, but extensive soaking will cause them to lose flavour.

cucumber and radish salsa
with crisp-skinned salmon .... serves 4

RADISHES ARE PEPPERY ROOT VEGETABLES RELATED TO THE MUSTARD PLANT. THERE ARE MANY VARIETIES, WHICH
MAY BE RED, BLACK OR WHITE (DAIKON). BUY SMOOTH, FIRM, SMALL RADISHES; LARGE ONES TEND TO BE TOUGH.
STORE THEM WITHOUT THEIR LEAVES, AS THESE ACCELERATE MOISTURE LOSS.

salsa

cucumber	1 large
celery	2 stalks, thinly sliced
French shallot	1, diced
avocado	1, diced
baby white and/or red radishes	20, halved, or quartered if large
coriander (cilantro)	1 small handful

dressing

olive oil	80 ml (2½ fl oz/⅓ cup)
lime juice	2 tablespoons
lime zest	1 teaspoon finely grated
garlic	1 clove, crushed
honey	1 teaspoon
salmon	4 small fillets, skin on
olive oil	2–3 tablespoons
coriander (cilantro)	1 small handful

To make the salsa, peel the cucumber and cut in half lengthways. Using a teaspoon, scoop out and discard the seeds. Slice very thinly into half-moon shapes and put in a large bowl. Add the celery, shallot, avocado, radishes and coriander.

To make the dressing, put the oil, lime juice, lime zest, garlic and honey in a small bowl and mix well. Season with salt and freshly ground black pepper, to taste.

Brush the salmon lightly with olive oil and sprinkle the skin with a little salt. Heat the remaining oil in a large frying pan over high heat. When hot, add the salmon, skin side down, and immediately hold a spatula or another frying pan on top of the fillets to keep them flat. Fry for 1–2 minutes, or until the skin is crisp and brown all over. Reduce the heat to medium and turn the salmon. Cook until just opaque, 2–3 minutes, depending on the thickness. Drain on paper towels.

When cool enough to handle, use kitchen scissors to cut each salmon fillet across the grain into 3 strips. Break each strip into bite-sized pieces of several flakes. Add to the salsa, along with the dressing and coriander. Toss gently to coat, and serve immediately.

Use a teaspoon to remove the seeds from the cucumber

Add the salmon, skin side down, to the frying pan

Using kitchen scissors, cut the salmon into strips

three ways with tomatoes

RIPE RED TOMATOES DRIPPING WITH JUICE AND BURSTING WITH FLAVOUR BEAR NO RELATION TO THE ANAEMIC SPECIMENS THAT TOO OFTEN TURN UP ON SUPERMARKET SHELVES. SEEK OUT THE REAL, SUN-RIPENED DEAL FOR A REVELATION. SWEET CHERRY TOMATOES ARE DIVINE PAIRED WITH SPICY CHORIZO. WHILE TOMATOES ARE IN SEASON, MAKE THE MOST OF THE HARVEST. DRY YOUR OWN WITH SICHUAN SPICES FOR SOMETHING DIFFERENT, OR ROAST TOMATOES FOR YOUR OWN PASTA SAUCE — A WORTHWHILE LABOUR OF LOVE.

cherry tomato and chorizo migas

Cut the crusts off 4 thick slices of 2-day-old bread and cut the bread into 2 cm (3/4 inch) cubes. Cut 1 chorizo into pieces of a similar size to the bread cubes. Heat 80 ml (2 1/2 fl oz/1/3 cup) olive oil in a large frying pan over high heat. Add the chorizo, 250 g (9 oz) yellow cherry tomatoes, a large pinch of paprika, a pinch of chilli flakes and 1/2 teaspoon cumin seeds. Fry, stirring often, for 4 minutes, or until browned. Add 2 crushed garlic cloves and fry for 20 seconds. Remove the chorizo mixture from the pan with a slotted spoon and drain on paper towels. Add the bread to the pan and fry for about 4 minutes, until crisp and golden, then remove with a slotted spoon and drain on paper towels. When all the ingredients have cooled, combine in a serving bowl. Serve with toothpicks and napkins. Serves 4.

sichuan oven-dried tomatoes

Cut 12 roma (plum) tomatoes in half lengthways and place cut side up on a wire rack in a baking tray. Coarsely grind 1 teaspoon sichuan pepper in a spice grinder and sprinkle over the tomatoes with 3/4 teaspoon salt flakes. Roast in a preheated 130°C (250°F/ Gas 1) oven for 3 hours, or until dry but still soft. Toss with 1 tablespoon oil, 2 teaspoons sesame oil and 1/2 teaspoon toasted sesame seeds. Store in the refrigerator in a sealed container for up to 5 days. Makes 24 pieces.

roast tomato sauce on penne

Cut a cross in the base of 750 g (1 lb 10 oz) roma (plum) tomatoes. Put in a heatproof bowl and cover with boiling water. Leave for 30 seconds then transfer to cold water and peel the skin away from the cross. Cut the tomatoes into 1–2 cm (1/2–3/4 inch) cubes. Squeeze out the juice and put the tomato to a shallow ovenproof dish. Add 2 crushed garlic cloves, 1 tablespoon chopped basil, a pinch of cayenne pepper and 2 tablespoons olive oil. Season with salt and freshly ground black pepper and mix well. Combine 30 g (1 oz/1/3 cup) fresh breadcrumbs and 30 g (1 oz/1/3 cup) grated pecorino cheese and scatter evenly over the tomato. Bake in a preheated 200°C (400°F/Gas 6) oven for 30 minutes, or until the top is golden and crusty. Meanwhile, cook 350 g (12 oz) penne in a saucepan of boiling salted water until *al dente* according to the manufacturer's instructions. Drain and return to the pan. Add 1 small handful torn basil and the tomato sauce, only breaking up the crust when the pasta and sauce are tossed together. Serves 4.

peperonata of yellow capsicums, anchovies and capers
serves 4

PEPERONATA IS A MOST ATTRACTIVE DISH, SERVED AS AN ACCOMPANIMENT TO A HOT SUMMER'S BARBECUE, OR AS A PART OF AN ANTIPASTI SPREAD. RED CAPSICUMS (PEPPERS) MAY BE SUBSTITUTED, OR USE A MIXTURE OF BOTH, BUT AVOID GREEN CAPSICUMS; THEY ARE UNRIPE, AND DO NOT HAVE THE NECESSARY SWEETNESS.

yellow capsicums (peppers)	4 large, quartered and seeded
olive oil	2 tablespoons
anchovy fillets	3, halved lengthways
baby capers in salt	2 teaspoons, unrinsed

Remove the membrane from the capsicum and press the quarters flat. Cook, skin side up, under a hot grill (broiler) until the skins blacken and blister. Cool in a plastic bag, then peel.

Put the capsicum in a shallow dish and drizzle with the olive oil. Toss in the anchovies and capers and set aside for 2–3 hours before serving. Store in the refrigerator for 5–7 days, but bring the mixture to room temperature before serving.

Although capsicums (also known as sweet or bell peppers) are fruits, they are more commonly used as a vegetable. Capsicums vary in appearance but they are all basically smooth, shiny and hollow, and contain thin white membranes and small seeds. Capsicums start off green, then ripen to red, yellow, orange or even purple-black, depending on the variety. Red, yellow and golden capsicums are the ones that have taken longest to ripen, and this is reflected in both their sweetness and their price. Choose fruits that are free of wrinkles or soft spots, and store in the refrigerator crisper for up to 1 week. Cut capsicums should be wrapped in paper rather than plastic, which will make them sweat and perish.

eggplant

choosing

Eggplant (aubergine, melanzane, brinjal) comes in many shapes and colours, but the one that is favoured for grilling is the handsome egg-shaped purple variety. Look for a smooth skin without dimples, a uniformly firm flesh, a bright-green stem base and an obvious ridge running down one side.

preparing

Avoid stainless steel utensils and non-aluminium pans, as these will discolor the flesh. When slices are called for, the skin is normally left on, as this supports the flesh and holds a slice together. However, some recipes, especially those that cube the flesh, will call for the eggplant to be peeled.

Eggplant has a high water content, which carries a bitterness when immature or old. It is common practice to salt sliced eggplant to draw these bitter juices. This degorgement also reduces the amount of oil required for frying or grilling. Another step to minimize the oil used when frying is to lightly flour the slices. Flouring will also help to achieve a crisp outside with a moist but firm inside.

frying

Asian cooks tend to prefer a flavourless vegetable oil, while Mediterranean cooking uses olive oil for its complementary flavour. In a large frying pan or wok, heat 3 tablespoons of oil to medium–high. Add eggplant slices or cubes in batches and fry, turning to each side once, until crisp and golden, about 2 minutes each side. Add more oil as needed. When using a chargrill pan, brush or spray slices with oil and fry over a high heat until well marked, 4–5 minutes each side.

grilling

Eggplant is enhanced by the smokiness grilling creates. Brushing with oil further adds to the flavour, and it enriches the colour and keeps the flesh moist. Cut the eggplant into 1.5 cm ($5/8$ inch) slices. Brush with oil and arrange on the grill plate of a medium–hot barbecue, chargrill or grill (broiler). Grill until tender and golden brown, 4–5 minutes on each side. Brush with more oil if you like, but avoid turning the slices more than once. If you intend using a flavoured oil or extra virgin olive oil, brush onto the eggplant after it has been grilled, but while it is still hot.

baby squash baked in the barbecue

NO OTHER COOKING METHOD SAYS SUMMER MORE ELOQUENTLY THAN BARBECUING. HERE, MELTINGLY TENDER BARBECUED BABY SQUASH AND DELICATE BABY SPINACH ARE TUMBLED IN A CREAMY, CITRUSY DRESSING FOR A COLOURFUL SUMMER SIDE DISH OR LIGHT LUNCH.

yellow baby (pattypan) or scallop squash	12
olive oil	60 ml (2 fl oz/¼ cup)
crème fraîche	1½ tablespoons
orange juice	1 tablespoon
orange zest	½ teaspoon grated
mint	1 teaspoon chopped, plus 1 small handful leaves
baby English spinach leaves	1 small handful
rocket (arugula)	1 small handful

Preheat one burner of a covered barbecue to medium heat. Put the squash in a foil baking tray and toss with half the olive oil. Season with salt and pepper. Place the tray on a rack over the unlit burner in the barbecue, close the lid and bake by indirect heat for 30–35 minutes, or until tender. (Alternatively, you can cook the squash in a preheated 180°C (350°F/Gas 4) oven.)

Meanwhile, put the remaining olive oil, crème fraîche, orange juice, orange zest and chopped mint in a small bowl and mix until smooth. Season with salt and freshly ground black pepper.

Cut the squash in half and put in a bowl with the mint leaves, spinach and rocket. Add the dressing and toss to coat. Serve immediately, while the squash are still warm.

Toss the squash in half of the olive oil until well coated

Mix together the dressing ingredients until smooth

zucchini madeleines ....makes 24

zucchini (courgettes)	2 small (250 g/9 oz total weight)
butter	60 g (2¼ oz), softened
raw caster (superfine) sugar	160 g (5½ oz/¾ cup)
egg	1
pecans	40 g (1½ oz/⅓ cup), roasted and finely chopped
self-raising flour	125 g (4½ oz/1 cup)
ground nutmeg	½ teaspoon
ground cinnamon	¼ teaspoon

Preheat the oven to 180°C (350°F/Gas 4). Grease a 12-hole madeleine tin. Coarsely grate the zucchini, then squeeze out the excess liquid with your hands.

Stir the butter into the sugar. Add the egg, beating well. Stir in the zucchini and pecans. Sift in the flour, nutmeg, cinnamon and a pinch of salt and gently fold through the zucchini mixture. Using half the mixture, spoon a rounded tablespoon into each hole of the prepared tin.

Bake for 15 minutes, or until golden. Cool in the tin for 5 minutes before turning out. Repeat with the remaining mixture.

When cool, pile in heaps on serving plates to serve.

Zucchini (courgettes) are baby marrows. They are one of the most versatile of vegetables, being delicious raw, cooked, stuffed, baked, fried, stewed or in fritters. There are myriad ways, from ratatouille to freshly baked zucchini bread, to make the most of this cheap and abundant ingredient. There are pale green, dark green and yellow varieties. Baby zucchini lend themselves perfectly to fresh, raw and lightly cooked dishes, while their larger, older siblings are definitely the go for heartier, slow-cooked dishes. When shopping, look for firm, unblemished zucchini. Eat as soon as possible after purchase, as refrigeration makes the texture deteriorate. There is no need to peel them; in fact, most of the flavour is in the skin.

tomato and pecan upside-down cake

. . . . makes a 20 cm (8 inch) cake

BOTANICALLY A FRUIT, TOMATOES ARE USUALLY USED AS A VEGETABLE. THIS RECIPE, HOWEVER, HONOURS THEIR TRUE NATURE AND TEAMS THEM WITH PECANS AND SPICES FOR AN UNUSUAL CAKE. THE TOMATOES CHANGE RADICALLY TO BECOME LUSCIOUS AND PLUMP, AND THE JUICES CARAMELIZE TO A RICH TOFFEE-LIKE COATING.

roma (plum) tomatoes	4 firm
pecans	12
unsalted butter	175 g (6 oz), melted
fresh ginger	1 teaspoon grated
light brown sugar	175 g (6 oz/1 cup firmly packed)
golden syrup or dark corn syrup	90 g (3¼ oz/¼ cup)
plain (all-purpose) flour	185 g (6½ oz/1½ cups)
baking powder	1½ teaspoons
ground ginger	3 teaspoons
ground allspice	¼ teaspoon
thick (double/heavy) cream	to serve

Preheat the oven to 180°C (350°F/Gas 4). Grease and flour a 22 cm (8½ inch) spring-form tin. Cut the core from each tomato and score a cross in the base. Put in a heatproof bowl and cover with boiling water. Leave for 30 seconds then transfer to cold water and peel the skin away from the cross. Cut the tomatoes lengthways into 1 cm (½ inch) slices. Squeeze gently to get rid of the juice and some of the seeds; don't worry about those seeds that don't detach easily. Arrange the tomato slices, cut side down, in a spoke pattern in the prepared tin. Fill in the larger gaps with half the pecans.

Finely chop the remaining pecans and mix them with 1 table-spoon of the melted butter, the grated ginger and 70 g (2½ oz/⅓ cup) of the brown sugar in a small bowl. Scatter evenly over the tomato.

Combine the golden syrup, 125 ml (4 fl oz/½ cup) water and the remaining butter in a saucepan and heat until smooth.

Sift the flour, baking powder, ground ginger and allspice into a large bowl. Stir in the remaining brown sugar, then gradually add the golden syrup mixture and mix until smooth. Spread over the tomato and shake the tin firmly once or twice to ensure that the mixture fills the gaps around the tomato.

Bake on the middle shelf for 35–40 minutes, or until a skewer comes out clean when inserted into the centre of the cake. Remove from the oven and run a knife around the edge to loosen the cake. Without removing the cake, invert the tin onto a flat plate and leave to cool for 15 minutes before removing the side of the tin. Serve warm with cream.

Layer the tomato slices in the base of the prepared tin

Scatter the pecan and sugar mixture evenly over the tomatoes

autumn

Autumn is the season of 'mists and mellow fruitfulness', a time of reflection and reconnection after the social whirl of summer. As the days shorten and each evening becomes a little crisper than the last, there comes a yearning for the slow and earthy in all things. Nature has a keener edge as the glitter of summer gives way to the nostalgia of autumnal days. Weekends become about camping under the trees and rambling through the woods, and the beach is left to the intrepid. Before our thoughts, and the seasons, turn to the barren months of winter there is one final glorious burst of bounteous fertility as plants make a last-ditch effort to fruit and flower before the cold sets in. This is our chance to slow down in the kitchen and savour the deep, complex flavours of autumn.

The meeting point of summer and winter, autumn straddles the gap between the extremes. Autumn food occupies the same space in our hearts. More substantial than the fast, light dishes of summer, yet still simple; sumptuous and filling, yet not as heavy as the classics of winter — it's about taking the best that nature has to offer and then treating it simply to draw out its essence.

In these mild, darkening months, fields and forests offer an abundance of wild mushrooms; garlic, leeks and onions are at their freshest and sweetest; potatoes, turnips, parsnips and swedes are ready to be pulled from the earth; beetroot, broccoli and borlotti beans are fresh and ready to cook. There is no easier way to judge what is truly in season than to visit your local farmers' market. Even if it's not possible for you to regularly frequent a farmers' market, a visit there will prove an educative and fascinating experience, allowing you to confidently select those vegetables which are truly in season during your weekly supermarket shop.

To bring out the purest flavour of each dish, all you need is a little knowledge and a sure hand. Every cooking technique has its place; it's simply a matter of deciding on the effect you want and treating the vegetable appropriately. Autumn vegetables are versatile, lending themselves to a number of dishes and styles. Beans can be briefly blanched for a warm salad or stewed with tomatoes for a hearty dish; mushrooms can be grilled, fried or baked; and there's almost no end to the culinary uses of the humble yet beloved potato.

So gather the autumn harvest to your heart — this is the season to embrace fecundity and make each meal a generous feast. Let nature set the menu and revel in fresh, seasonal vegetables treated with care and served with love.

cauliflower bhajis with cucumber raita

AT ITS BEST IN AUTUMN, GOOD CAULIFLOWER WILL HAVE COMPACT, TIGHT WHITE HEADS WITH NO BLEMISHES OR DISCOLORATION. IT WILL ONLY NEED BRIEF COOKING TO GIVE A CRISP TEXTURE AND TO BRING OUT THE FLAVOUR. OUT OF SEASON, THE FLORETS IN THIS RECIPE WILL NEED TO BE BLANCHED FOR 1 MINUTE BEFORE BATTERING.

raita

Lebanese (short) cucumber	1 small
plain yoghurt	200 g (7 oz/heaped $^3/_4$ cup)
mint	1 tablespoon chopped
turmeric	a pinch

batter

plain (all-purpose) flour	185 g (6$^1/_2$ oz/1$^1/_2$ cups)
bicarbonate of soda	1 teaspoon
ground coriander	1 teaspoon
garam masala	1 teaspoon
turmeric	$^1/_2$ teaspoon
chilli powder	$^1/_4$ teaspoon
coriander (cilantro)	2 tablespoons chopped
cauliflower florets	300 g (10$^1/_2$ oz/2$^1/_2$ cups)
oil	for deep-frying

To make the raita, grate the cucumber and place in a sieve over a bowl. Sprinkle with $^1/_4$ teaspoon salt and set aside to drain for 20 minutes. Squeeze out any excess liquid. Combine the cucumber with the yoghurt, mint and turmeric.

To make the batter, sift the flour and bicarbonate of soda into a bowl and stir in the ground coriander, garam masala, turmeric, chilli powder and chopped coriander. Mix well. Gradually stir in 185 ml (6 fl oz/$^3/_4$ cup) water and mix to a smooth paste. Add another 125 ml (4 fl oz/$^1/_2$ cup) water, a little at a time, until the batter reaches the consistency of custard. Add the cauliflower and toss to coat.

Heat the oil in a deep saucepan to 180°C (350°F) or until a cube of bread browns in 30 seconds. Using tongs, shake off the excess batter from the florets and lower them into the oil, a few at a time. Fry for about 1 minute, until golden brown. Remove with a slotted spoon and drain on paper towels. Serve immediately, accompanied by the raita.

Squeeze the excess water out of the grated cucumber

Add water until batter reaches the consistency of custard

Fry the florets, a few at a time, until golden brown

open lasagne of mushrooms, pine nuts and thyme

.... serves 4

USE YOUR FAVOURITE TYPE OF CAP MUSHROOMS, SUCH AS CHESTNUT, SWISS BROWN, PORTOBELLO OR EVEN SHIITAKE, AS LONG AS THEY ARE NO BIGGER THAN 4 CM (1½ INCHES) ACROSS. TO PREPARE, CUT OFF THE DIRTY END OF THE STALKS, SHAKE OFF EXCESS SOIL AND LEAVES AND WIPE THE CAPS WITH A DAMP CLOTH.

fresh pasta sheets	200 g (7 oz) (2 medium)
butter	80 g (2¾ oz/⅓ cup)
olive oil	1 tablespoon
assorted mushrooms	300 g (10½ oz/3⅓ cups), sliced
lean bacon	2 slices, cut into pieces of similar size to the mushroom slices
garlic	2 cloves, finely sliced
fresh thyme	1 tablespoon
pine nuts	1 tablespoon, toasted
thick (heavy/double) cream	3 tablespoons
extra virgin olive oil	3 tablespoons
pecorino pepato cheese	35 g (1¼ oz/⅓ cup) coarsely shredded (or use grana padano)

Put a large saucepan of water on to boil for the pasta and add 1 teaspoon of salt. Cut the lasagne sheets into sixteen 8 cm (3¼ inch) squares. Boil 8 of the squares for 4 minutes, or until *al dente*. Transfer with a slotted spoon to a bowl of cold water. After 15–20 seconds, they should be cool enough to handle. Lay flat on a dry tea towel and cover with another tea towel. It doesn't matter that the squares may have cooked to uneven sizes. Repeat with the remaining pasta squares.

Heat the butter and olive oil in a large frying pan. Fry the mushrooms and bacon over a high heat, stirring often, until golden brown, 3–4 minutes. Add the garlic and thyme and fry for 1 minute. Add the pine nuts, cream and 2 tablespoons of extra virgin olive oil and stir until combined. Remove from the heat and season with freshly ground black pepper. Taste for salt.

Preheat the griller to medium–high. Place a pasta square in each of 4 shallow pasta bowls. Cover with a heaped tablespoon of mushroom mixture. Repeat twice more then top with the last 4 pasta squares. The pasta doesn't have to be in uniform stacks, nor the piles neat.

Drizzle the remaining extra virgin olive oil over the top and scatter with the pecorino pepato. Place the bowls under the heat just long enough for the cheese to start to melt. Serve hot or warm.

Boil the pasta squares, in batches, until al dente

Fry the mushrooms and bacon until golden brown

Compile stacks of pasta sheets and mushroom mixture

leeks with scallops in their shell............................serves 4

THE WONDERFUL FLESH OF SEA SCALLOPS REQUIRES A LIGHT HAND AND GENTLE COOKING. WHETHER TO USE THE CORAL (ROE) IS A MATTER OF PREFERENCE; SOME LOVE THE SLIGHTLY STRONGER FLAVOUR AND VISUAL APPEAL THAT IT BRINGS TO A DISH, WHILE OTHERS FEEL THAT IT DETRACTS FROM THE SUBTLETY OF THE WHITE FLESH.

scallops on the shell	12, coral optional
butter	30 g (1 oz)
leeks	6 medium, white part only, thinly sliced
chervil	2 sprigs, plus 1 small handful leaves
dry white wine	125 ml (4 fl oz/1/2 cup)
freshly ground nutmeg	to serve

Remove the scallops from their shells. Wash the shells and leave to dry. Discard the dark vein from the scallops.

Heat the butter in a medium frying pan over low heat. Add the leek and chervil sprigs and fry for 8–10 minutes, or until soft but not browned. Add the wine, increase the heat to medium and simmer for 1 minute. Season with salt and freshly ground white pepper, and a small grind of nutmeg.

Remove the pan from the heat and discard the chervil sprigs. Rest the pan at an angle and move the leek to the high side, letting the pan juices drain down. Divide the leek among the scallop shells, making a little pile in the centre.

Add the scallops to the pan and cook over medium heat, turning once, for about 1 minute, until opaque. Put the scallops on top of the leek and spoon a little of the pan juices over them. Top with the chervil leaves and serve warm.

As with all of the alliums, or members of the onion family, leeks make a wonderful base for other dishes, but their mild though distinctive flavour also makes them worthy of the starring role. Baby leeks are particularly tender and are delicious braised or roasted whole, or shredded finely for a salad. Bigger leeks are wonderful used alongside or in place of onion and are essential in a vichyssoise. It's important to wash leeks thoroughly, as dirt can remain trapped in their many layers. To prepare, cut off the leaves, slice vertically down through the stem of the leek and fan the layers out under cold running water. Use only the white part of the leek unless the recipe advises otherwise.

daikon with sashimi .... serves 4

DAIKON, OR WHITE RADISH, HAS A SUBTLE TASTE, MUCH MILDER THAN THAT OF ITS LITTLE RED COUSIN. IT IS PARTICULARLY APPRECIATED IN JAPAN. HERE, ENHANCED BY ASIAN FLAVOURS, DAIKON APPEARS IN A SALAD TO COMPLEMENT SASHIMI.

dipping sauce

Japanese soy sauce	125 ml (4 fl oz/1/2 cup)
fresh ginger	1 teaspoon grated
sugar	a pinch

daikon salad

daikon	150 g (5 1/2 oz), peeled
Lebanese (short) cucumber	1
carrot	1, peeled
ginger	4 cm (1 1/2 inch) piece
spring onions (scallions)	3, thinly sliced on the diagonal
sesame seeds	1/2 teaspoon, roasted
rice vinegar	2 teaspoons
Japanese soy sauce	2 teaspoons
mirin	2 teaspoons
nori	1 sheet, roasted

sashimi-quality salmon	250 g (9 oz) piece
sashimi-quality tuna	250 g (9 oz) piece
wasabi paste	to serve

To make the dipping sauce, stir the soy sauce, ginger and sugar in a small bowl until the sugar has dissolved. Divide the sauce among 4 small dishes and place on 4 serving plates.

To make the salad, shave the daikon, cucumber and carrot lengthways into wide thin strips with a mandolin or a vegetable peeler and put in a large bowl. Cut the ginger into fine matchsticks and add to the bowl.

Just before you are ready to serve, add the spring onion, sesame seeds, rice vinegar, soy sauce and mirin and toss to coat. Divide the salad among the serving plates. Cut the nori into thin strips using scissors and scatter some over each salad. Using a very sharp knife, slice the salmon and tuna into even 5 mm (1/4 inch) thick strips. Divide among the plates, arranging them in neat rows. Add a dab of wasabi to the plates and serve immediately.

Also known as Japanese horseradish or mooli, daikon looks like a bigger, uglier, knobblier parsnip and, if its flavour can be likened to anything, it is reminiscent of a finer, less fiery radish. To capitalize on the intense flavour of daikon, try eating it raw; it's wonderful grated over tofu or shredded into a salad. Daikon also responds very well to being cooked slowly, turning soft and mellow as it absorbs the cooking juices. Choose firm, smooth and slightly shiny daikon, as this is a good indication that it is fresh. Remove their green tops and store wrapped in plastic in the vegetable crisper of the fridge. If eating raw, use within 3–4 days. Daikon will last for up to 1 week if you intend to cook it.

spicy pumpkin, chickpeas and salami...serves 4

THIS DISH PERFECTLY HIGHLIGHTS THE ABILITY OF PUMPKIN (SQUASH) TO CARRY STRONG FLAVOURS. CHOOSE PUMPKINS THAT ARE HEAVY FOR THEIR SIZE AND HAVE UNBLEMISHED SKINS. STORE WHOLE AT ROOM TEMPERATURE FOR UP TO 1 MONTH. WRAP CUT PUMPKIN IN PLASTIC WRAP AND STORE IN THE REFRIGERATOR.

dried chickpeas	350 g (12 oz/1²/₃ cups)
salami, such as milanese	80 g (2³/₄ oz) sliced
pumpkin (winter squash)	750 g (1 lb 10 oz), peeled to give 500 g (1 lb 2 oz)
tomato	1 large
oil	2 tablespoons
garlic	3 cloves, crushed
fresh ginger	1 tablespoon grated
medium red chilli	¹/₂, seeded and finely chopped
garam masala	3 teaspoons
ground coriander	3 teaspoons
turmeric	2 teaspoons
black cumin seeds	1 teaspoon
tomato passata (puréed tomatoes)	250 ml (9 fl oz/1 cup)
lemon juice	1 tablespoon
coriander (cilantro)	1 large handful leaves

Soak the chickpeas in cold water overnight. Drain and put in a large saucepan with plenty of cold water. Bring to the boil, then reduce the heat and simmer for about 1¹/₂ hours, or until tender. Drain the chickpeas.

Cut each slice of salami into 3 strips. Cut the pumpkin into 2–2.5 cm (³/₄–1 inch) cubes. Cut the core from the tomato and score a cross in the base. Put in a heatproof bowl and cover with boiling water. Leave for 30 seconds, then transfer to cold water and peel the skin away from the cross. Dice the flesh. Squeeze out and discard the excess juice and seeds.

Heat half the oil in a large heavy-based saucepan over high heat and fry the salami for about 2 minutes, until lightly browned. Remove with tongs and drain on paper towels.

Reduce the heat to medium, add the remaining oil and fry the garlic, ginger, chilli, garam masala, ground coriander, turmeric and cumin seeds for 2 minutes. Stir in the pumpkin, then add enough warm water to cover. Bring to the boil, then reduce the heat and simmer, stirring occasionally, for 7–8 minutes. Stir in the tomato, tomato passata and chickpeas and simmer for 5 minutes, or until the pumpkin is tender and most of the liquid has evaporated. Season with salt and freshly ground pepper, to taste. Remove from the heat and set aside for 5 minutes. Add the lemon juice, coriander leaves and salami and toss through.

Fry the salami strips until lightly browned

Add the pumpkin to the spice mixture and stir to coat

three ways with beetroot

FOR THOSE WHO KNOW BEETROOT ONLY FROM TINS, TRYING THE FRESH VARIETY WILL OPEN YOUR EYES TO A WHOLE NEW WORLD. THE DEPTH OF FLAVOUR CONTAINED IN THESE SCARLET GLOBES CAN ONLY BE CAPTURED IF YOU START WITH A SUEDE-SKINNED RAW BEETROOT. BABY BEETS ARE THE SWEETEST AND ARE PERFECT WITH TATSOI AND A SWEET-TANGY DRESSING. ROASTING THEM WITH A WHOLE BULB OF GARLIC ADDS A SMOKY DEPTH, OR TRY THIS ZESTY CITRUS GLAZE TO COMPLEMENT AND YET CUT THROUGH THE SWEETNESS AT THE SAME TIME.

baby beetroot and tatsoi salad with honey mustard dressing

Wearing rubber gloves, trim 1.6 kg (3 lb 8 oz/2 bunches) baby beetroot, discarding the stalks but reserving the unblemished leaves. Bring a medium saucepan of water to the boil. Add the beetroot and simmer, covered, for 8–10 minutes, or until tender, then drain. Ease off the skins, pat dry with paper towels and rinse. Put the beetroot in a large shallow bowl. Bring a small saucepan of water to the boil. Add a large pinch of salt and 250 g (9 oz/1²/₃ cups) broad (fava) beans (from 500 g (1 lb 2 oz/3 cups) fresh broad beans in the pod) and simmer for 2–3 minutes, then drain. When cool enough to handle, slip the beans out of their skins and add to the beetroot. Add the reserved beetroot leaves and the small inner leaves of 200 g (7 oz/1 bunch) tatsoi. To make the dressing, put 80 ml (2½ fl oz/¹/₃ cup) olive oil and 1 tablespoon each of lemon juice, wholegrain mustard and honey in a small bowl and whisk well to combine. Season with salt and freshly ground black pepper, to taste. Pour over the beetroot mixture and toss gently. Serve warm or at room temperature. Serves 4.

roasted beetroot and whole garlic

Line a roasting tin with baking paper. Wearing rubber gloves, trim the tops off 3 small beetroot, leaving 5 cm (2 inches) of the stalks intact. Thinly peel the beetroot and cut them in half lengthways. Arrange, cut side up, in the prepared tin. Combine 1 tablespoon balsamic vinegar and 100 ml (3½ fl oz) olive oil and drizzle half over the beetroot. Season lightly with salt and freshly ground black pepper. Wrap 12 unpeeled garlic cloves in a small sheet of foil and add to the tin. Roast in a preheated 180°C (350°F/Gas 4) oven for 50 minutes, then cover loosely with foil and bake for a further 45 minutes, or until the beetroot is tender. Unwrap the garlic and gently squeeze the flesh out from 1 clove. Add to the remaining dressing and mix in with a fork. Transfer the beetroot to a serving dish and drizzle with the garlic dressing. Scatter the remaining garlic cloves around and serve immediately. Serves 4.

orange-glazed beetroot with dill

Wearing rubber gloves, trim 750 g (1 lb 10 oz) small beetroot and put in a large saucepan of cold water. Cover and bring to the boil over high heat. Reduce the heat to medium and simmer, partly covered, for 15 minutes, or until tender, then drain. Meanwhile, heat 1 tablespoon olive oil in a large frying pan. Add 1 teaspoon each of dill seeds and ground cumin and stir over medium heat for 20–25 seconds, or until aromatic. Add 250 ml (9 fl oz/1 cup) orange juice, increase the heat and boil for 5–6 minutes, or until reduced by half. Peel the beetroot, then cut each into 4 wedges. Add to the frying pan with 20 g (³/₄ oz) butter and cook, stirring often, for 2–3 minutes. Stir in 2 teaspoons chopped dill and the grated zest of half a small orange. Serve hot or at room temperature. Serves 4.

tagine of fennel, red onions and dutch carrots with couscous . . . . serves 4

IN NORTH AFRICA, AND PARTICULARLY IN MOROCCO, A TAGINE IS AN EARTHENWARE DISH WITH A CONICAL LID IN WHICH STEWS ARE SIMMERED. THE STEWS, ALSO CALLED TAGINES, ARE CHARACTERIZED BY HAVING BOTH SAVOURY AND SWEET FLAVOURS. THEY ARE SERVED WITH COUSCOUS, AS HERE, OR RICE.

baby fennel bulbs	3
red onions	6 small (about 80 g/2³/4 oz each)
Dutch or baby carrots	8
chicken stock	375 ml (13 fl oz/1¹/2 cups)
ground ginger	1 teaspoon
ground cumin	1 scant teaspoon
ground cinnamon	¹/2 teaspoon
honey	1¹/2 tablespoons
garlic	5 cloves
cinnamon stick	1
currants	2 tablespoons
mint	1 small handful

saffron couscous

saffron threads	a small pinch
chicken stock or water	625 ml (22 fl oz/2¹/2 cups)
instant couscous	375 g (13 oz/2 cups)
butter	50 g (1³/4 oz)

Trim the tops off the fennel, leaving 2–3 cm (³/4–1¹/4 inches) of stalks remaining, and discard the tough outer leaves. Halve the fennel lengthways. Peel the onions, leaving the ends intact. Trim the carrots, leaving 1–2 cm (¹/2–³/4 inch) of stalks remaining. Scrub the carrots.

Put the stock in a flameproof casserole dish and add the fennel, onions, carrots, ground ginger, cumin, cinnamon, honey, garlic and cinnamon stick. Bring to the boil, then add the currants. Cover and simmer over low heat for 20–25 minutes, or until the vegetables are soft. Toss the mint leaves through the tagine.

Meanwhile, to make the saffron couscous, soak the saffron in 2 tablespoons hot water for 10 minutes. Bring the stock to the boil in a medium saucepan. Stir in the couscous and saffron with its soaking liquid. Cover and cook for 3 minutes. Remove from the heat and set aside for 5 minutes. Add the butter and toss with a fork to loosen the grains. Serve with the vegetables.

Halve the trimmed fennel bulbs lengthways

Add the vegetables and cinnamon stick to the pot

Stir the saffron and soaking water into the couscous and stock

sweet potato filo pie .... serves 8

WITH ITS RUFFLED EDGES LOOKING LIKE LAYERS OF TISSUE PAPER, THIS IS A STUNNING PIE FOR A SPECIAL OCCASION. THE LOOSE-BASED RECTANGULAR TART TIN IS USED PURELY FOR ITS REMOVABLE BASE, AND TO CONTROL THE SHAPE OF THE PIE. THE FLUTED SIDES OF THE TIN AREN'T UTILIZED.

orange sweet potato	750 g (1 lb 10 oz), peeled
French shallots	12 small, peeled
baby potatoes	6, peeled and halved
olive oil	125 ml (4 fl oz/1/2 cup)
sweet paprika	1 teaspoon
ground ginger	1 teaspoon
ground cumin	2 teaspoons
ground cinnamon	1/4 teaspoon
baby English spinach	100 g (31/2 oz/2 cups)
sultanas (golden raisins)	60 g (21/4 oz/1/2 cup)
slivered almonds	85 g (3 oz/2/3 cup) toasted
pistachio kernels	100 g (31/2 oz/2/3 cup), coarsely chopped
coriander (cilantro)	40 g (1 cup) leaves, coarsely chopped
golden syrup or maple syrup	21/2 tablespoons
plain yoghurt	80 g (23/4 oz/1/3 cup)
canned chickpeas	400 g (14 oz), drained
garlic	3 cloves, finely chopped
cayenne pepper	a pinch
lemon juice	60 ml (2 fl oz/1/4 cup)
butter	125 g (41/2 oz), melted
filo pastry	9 sheets

Preheat the oven to 200°C (400°F/Gas 6). Cut the sweet potato into 2.5 cm (1 inch) cubes and put in a large roasting tin, along with the French shallots and baby potatoes. Combine the olive oil, paprika, ginger, cumin and cinnamon in a small bowl and pour over the vegetables. Toss to coat. Roast for 25 minutes, then turn the vegetables and roast for a further 15 minutes. Remove from the oven and reduce the oven temperature to 180°C (350°F/Gas 4). Put a baking tray in the oven.

Add the spinach and sultanas to the vegetables. Toss lightly, then set aside for 5 minutes for the spinach to wilt. Transfer to a large bowl and add the almonds, pistachios and coriander.

Put 2 tablespoons of the golden syrup, the yoghurt, chickpeas, garlic, cayenne and lemon juice in a food processor and blend until smooth. Season with salt and pepper, to taste. Add to the vegetables and mix through.

Lightly dampen a tea towel and use it to cover the sheets of filo as you work. Brush a 28 x 21 cm (111/4 x 81/4 inch) loose-based rectangular tart tin with butter. Brush a sheet of filo with butter and lay it on point over one end of the tin, so that three of the points stick out and the overhang at the end is about 10 cm (4 inches). Don't push the pastry into the rippled sides of the tin, just place it loosely on top. Brush another sheet of filo with butter and lay it similarly, at the opposite end of the tin. Brush a third sheet with butter and lay it in the middle of the tin. Continue in this way twice more, until all the filo is used.

Pile the sweet potato mixture in the centre of the tin. Starting in the middle, bring the opposite sides of the filo together, encasing the filling tightly but with the filo points sticking up (a little like a cloth around a Christmas pudding, tied at the top). Brush carefully with the remaining butter and drizzle the remaining golden syrup in zigzags over the top. Place on the baking tray and bake for 30 minutes, or until golden. Set aside for 5 minutes before serving.

Lay the pastry loosely in the tart tin; do not press it into the sides

Encase the filling with the pastry, letting the filo points stick up

three ways with spinach

FRESH, LEAFY SPINACH HAS A CERTAIN DARK AND LOAMY ESSENCE. IT'S ALMOST AS THOUGH YOU CAN TASTE THE IRON THAT MAKES IT SO GOOD FOR YOU. IT'S EASY TO BRING OUT THE BEST IN SPINACH WHEN IT'S SIMPLY STIR-FRIED WITH SMOKED TOFU AND ASIAN GREENS. BAKED WITH EGGS, SPRING ONIONS AND PROVOLONE, SPINACH BECOMES A SOFT SWIRL OF NOURISHING WHOLESOMENESS. TOSSED THROUGH HOT SPAGHETTI WITH PINE NUTS AND PANCETTA, THE GENTLY WILTED LEAVES BRINGS A FERROUS TANG TO THE DISH.

stir-fried spinach with tofu and asian greens

To make the dressing, put 2 tablespoons each of lime juice and vegetable oil, 1½ tablespoons fish sauce, 1 teaspoon sambal oelek and ½ teaspoon light brown sugar in a bowl and whisk well. Cut 200 g (7 oz) smoked tofu into 1.5–2 cm (⅝–¾ inch) cubes. Trim 400 g (14 oz/1 bunch) choy sum and cut it into 7–8 cm (2¾–3¼ inch) lengths. Heat 1 tablespoon oil in a large wok over medium heat and gently stir-fry the tofu for 2–3 minutes, or until golden brown. Add half the dressing and toss to coat. Remove from the wok and set aside. Add the choy sum to the wok and stir-fry for 1 minute. Add 150 g (5½ oz) torn English spinach and stir-fry for 1 minute. Return the tofu to the wok, add 2 teaspoons toasted sesame seeds and the remaining dressing and toss lightly. Serve with 1 small handful coriander (cilantro) leaves piled on top. Serves 4.

baked eggs and spinach

Heat 40 g (1½ oz) butter in a frying pan over high heat. Add 80 g (2¾ oz/2 cups) coarsely chopped English spinach and 4 thinly sliced spring onions (scallions). Cook, stirring, for 30–40 seconds, or until the spinach has wilted. Divide the spinach among 4 greased 150 ml (5 fl oz) ramekins. Beat 8 eggs with a pinch of nutmeg and season with salt and pepper. Pour over the spinach and sprinkle 2 tablespoons grated provolone or gouda cheese (optional) over the top. Transfer the ramekins to a roasting tin half filled with hot water. Bake in a preheated 180°C (350°F/Gas 4) oven for 25 minutes, or until the eggs are just set. Serves 4.

spaghetti with spinach, pine nuts and pancetta

Cook 350 g (12 oz) spaghetti in a large saucepan of boiling salted water until *al dente* according to the manufacturer's instructions. Slice 4 thin round slices of pancetta into 3 strips. Heat 60 ml (2 fl oz/¼ cup) oil in a large frying pan over medium heat and stir-fry the pancetta and 40 g (1½ oz/¼ cup) pine nuts for 1½–2 minutes, or until the pancetta is crisp and the nuts are golden. Stir in 60 g (2¼ oz/¼ cup) crème fraîche. Drain the pasta and add it to the pan. Add 100 g (3½ oz) English spinach, torn into small pieces, and toss well to coat. Serve drizzled with extra virgin olive oil (optional) and topped with parmesan shavings. Serves 4.

leek and chicken calzone................makes a 30 cm (12 inch) calzone

BUTTERMILK PASTRY IS A GOOD CHOICE FOR TURNOVERS AND CALZONE. IT IS STRONG ENOUGH TO SUPPORT A FILLING, YET SOFT AND BREAD-LIKE. IF MADE 24 HOURS IN ADVANCE, IT DEVELOPS A SOURDOUGH TASTE, GIVING THE FLAVOUR OF A YEAST DOUGH WITHOUT THE TIME INVOLVED.

pastry

plain (all-purpose) flour	280 g (10 oz/2¼ cups)
bicarbonate of soda (baking soda)	½ teaspoon
butter	20 g (¾ oz), chilled and cubed
buttermilk	170 ml (5½ fl oz/⅔ cup)

filling

butter	20 g (¾ oz)
oil	2 tablespoons
leeks	3 large, white part only, sliced
frozen soya beans	50 g (1¾ oz/⅓ cup), thawed
garlic	2 cloves, crushed
bacon	2 slices, cut into thin strips
chicken breast fillet	200 g (7 oz), cut into thick strips
fresh mozzarella (bocconcini)	80 g (2¾ oz), diced
basil	1 small handful, roughly torn
egg	1

To make the pastry, put the flour, bicarbonate of soda, ½ teaspoon salt and the butter in a food processor. Process in short bursts, using the pulse button, until the mixture is fine and crumbly. With the motor running, gradually add the buttermilk, stopping after the dough clumps into a ball. Transfer to a clean, dry work surface. The dough will be soft and just a little sticky, but try not to add extra flour. Knead for 1 minute, or until spongy and smooth. Cover with plastic wrap and set aside at room temperature for at least 30 minutes (or chill overnight).

To make the filling, heat the butter and half the oil in a large frying pan over medium–low heat and sauté the leek, without browning, for 7–8 minutes. Add the soya beans and garlic and cook for 1 minute. Transfer to a bowl. Add the remaining oil to the pan and sauté the bacon and chicken for 5–6 minutes, or until browned. Season with freshly ground black pepper and add to the leek mixture, along with the mozzarella and basil. Toss to combine.

Preheat the oven to 200°C (400°F/Gas 6) and put a baking sheet on the middle rack. Lightly beat the egg with 1 teaspoon water. Roll and stretch the dough out on a doubled sheet of baking paper to a 30 cm (12 inch) circle. Spread the filling over half the circle, leaving a 2 cm (¾ inch) border. Brush the border with the beaten egg. Using the baking paper for leverage, fold the uncovered dough over the filling to form a half-moon shape. Press the edges together and fold them over and in on themselves, giving a sealed rolled border. Pinch the edge into a pattern. Brush the calzone with beaten egg.

Using the baking paper as handles, transfer the calzone to the baking sheet in the oven. Bake for 20–25 minutes, or until golden brown. Remove from the oven and allow to stand for 5 minutes before serving.

Knead the dough until it is smooth and spongy

Fold the dough over the filling, using the paper for leverage

slow-cooked
catalonia chicory and pork . . . . serves 4

IN THIS SIMPLE AND HEARTY STEW FROM NORTHWESTERN SPAIN, THE CHICORY TENDERIZES THE PORK, MAKING THE DISH RICH AND MELLOW WITH JUST A SLIGHT BITTERNESS. THE LUSH GREEN TOPS OF YOUNG TURNIPS CAN BE USED INSTEAD OF THE CHICORY, AND CELERIAC CAN BE ADDED TO THE POT FOR A SAVOURY VARIATION.

chorizo	200 g (7 oz)
foreleg of pork	800 g (1 lb 12 oz)
olive oil	60 ml (2 fl oz/1/4 cup)
sweet paprika	3 teaspoons
chicken stock	1 litre (35 fl oz/4 cups)
Catalonia chicory	800 g (1 lb 12 oz/1 bunch)
potatoes	500 g (1 lb 2 oz), peeled and cut into large chunks

Cut the chorizo into large cubes. Cut the pork into 3–4 cm (1 1/4–1 1/2 inch) cubes.

Heat 1 tablespoon of the olive oil in a large heavy-based saucepan over high heat. Fry the chorizo for 3–4 minutes, or until browned. Remove from the pan and set aside.

Add the remaining oil to the pan and fry the pork over high heat for 6–8 minutes, or until browned. Sprinkle with the paprika, season well with salt and black pepper and stir to coat. Cook for 1 minute, then add the stock, bring to the boil and cover the pan. Reduce the heat and simmer for 30 minutes.

Slice the top 20 cm (8 inches) from the chicory, discarding the bottom half. Slice the chicory in half again to give 10 cm (4 inch) lengths. Add the chicory and chorizo to the pan, stirring well. Simmer, covered, for 20 minutes. Add the potato, cover and simmer for a further 30 minutes, removing the lid for the last 15 minutes. Check the seasoning before serving and serve with good crusty bread and a dish of green olives.

A tender, lightly bitter leaf, Catalonia chicory is one of various cultivated forms of wild chicory. It has been eaten for centuries across southern Europe and its romantic name suggests its origins. It became particularly popular in Italy, where it is known as cicoria catalogna, and it was introduced to the New World by Italian migrants. It is generally sold in fruit shops simply as chicory. The leaves resemble large dandelion leaves, and they can be braised, slow-cooked in stews and casseroles, or lightly boiled, dressed and served as a simple salad. As well as having an affinity with pork products, this type of chicory must surely owe part of its popularity to its ability to tenderize meat.

spinach and sweet potato salad
with orange-sesame dressing .... serves 4

SWEET POTATO AND ORANGE ARE ONE OF THOSE FOOD COMBINATIONS THAT ARE JUST MEANT TO GO TOGETHER. ROASTING OR GRILLING SWEET POTATO MAKES IT TENDER AND ENHANCES ITS SWEETNESS. THIS SALAD, WITH ITS CONTRAST OF SWEET AND TANGY, SOFT AND CRISP, IS EASY BUT IMPRESSIVE.

pitta bread	1
olive oil	3 tablespoons
orange sweet potato	500 g (1 lb 2 oz), unpeeled, cut into slices 1 cm (1/2 inch) thick
orange	1 small
baby spinach	150 g (51/2 oz)

dressing

olive oil	3 tablespoons
sesame oil	1 teaspoon
orange juice	2 tablespoons
lemon juice	1 teaspoon
orange zest	1 teaspoon finely grated
garlic	1 clove, crushed
dijon mustard	2 teaspoons

Preheat a grill (broiler) to high. Cut off and discard the edge of the pitta bread, split the bread into 2 thin halves, and lightly brush all over with some of the oil. Place under the grill and toast until crisp and lightly browned. Reserve.

Toss the sweet potato in the remaining oil and grill until soft and golden on both sides, 8–10 minutes. Transfer to a salad bowl.

Peel the orange, removing all the pith. To fillet the segments, hold the orange over a bowl and use a sharp knife to cut down either side of the membranes. Put the segments in the bowl and add the spinach. Break up the pitta crisps into small shards and put into the bowl. Toss lightly.

To make the dressing, put all the ingredients in a small bowl and whisk to blend. Season with salt and freshly ground black pepper, to taste. Pour over the salad just before serving.

Cut off the edge of the pitta bread, then split in half

Cut the orange segments away from the membrane

three ways with mushrooms

MUSHROOMS ARE ONE OF THE FEW REMAINING GIFTS OF NATURE'S WILD BOUNTY. THOSE IN THE KNOW TAKE TO THE WOODS EARLY IN THE DAY TO FIND THEIR OWN. MEATY MUSHROOMS MAKE A MEAL IN THEMSELVES. BAKE THEM WITH CREAMY RICOTTA FOR A SIMPLE, SUSTAINING COLD-DAY DISH. EASIER STILL, SAUTÉ WILD MUSHROOMS TO PILE HIGH ON GARLICKY BRUSCHETTA. FOR PERFECTLY SATISFYING PARTY FOOD, MAKE THESE DELICIOUS WONTONS WITH THEIR INTRIGUING MIX OF SLIPPERY MUSHROOMS AND DELICATE, CRUNCHY WATER CHESTNUTS.

individual pots of baked ricotta and mushrooms

Heat 20 g (3/4 oz) butter and 1 teaspoon oil in a small frying pan over high heat. Fry 125 g (41/2 oz) sliced button mushrooms and 1 crushed garlic clove briefly until lightly golden. Remove from the heat, add 1 teaspoon chopped marjoram, a pinch of ground nutmeg and salt and pepper, to taste. Brush four 125 ml (4 fl oz/1/2 cup) ramekins with a little extra virgin olive oil and line the bases with a circle of baking paper. Put the tip of a marjoram sprig in the base of each ramekin. Gently combine the mushrooms and 400 g (14 oz/2/3 cup) ricotta cheese. Divide among the ramekins and press the mixture down firmly. Bake in a preheated 180°C (350°F/Gas 4) oven for 20–25 minutes, or until the tops are crusty and the mixture has started to shrink from the sides of the ramekins. Cool for 5 minutes before turning out. Drizzle with extra virgin olive oil and serve hot, warm or cold. Serves 4. Note: Buy the ricotta for this recipe from a bulk block; it is much dryer and has a better texture than that sold in pre-weighed tubs.

sautéed mixed wild mushrooms with garlic bruschetta

Toast 4 slices of ciabatta under a hot grill (broiler) until golden brown. As soon as each side is done, rub it all over with the cut side of half a garlic clove. Heat 80 ml (21/2 fl oz/1/3 cup) olive oil in a large frying pan over medium heat and add 2 thinly sliced garlic cloves and a pinch of chilli flakes. Cook, stirring, for 10–15 seconds. Do not brown. Add 400 g (14 oz) mixed wild mushrooms, roughly chopped if large (or use mixed cultivated mushrooms and 5 g (1/8 oz) dried porcini that have been soaked in 100 ml (31/2 fl oz) hot water for 20 minutes). Increase the heat to high and cook for 1 minute. Add 100 ml (31/2 fl oz) vegetable stock (or, if you have used a mixture of cultivated and dried mushrooms, use the soaking water in place of stock) and cook for 2 minutes. Add 1 tablespoon chopped parsley, a large pinch of ground nutmeg and salt and freshly ground black pepper, to taste. Stir through 1 small handful flat-leaf (Italian) parsley. Serve hot, accompanied by the garlic bruschetta. Serves 4.

shiitake wontons with chilli ginger dipping sauce

To make the dipping sauce, combine 2 teaspoons grated fresh ginger, 11/2 teaspoons sweet chilli sauce, 100 ml (31/2 fl oz) light soy sauce, 2 tablespoons rice wine and 1/2 teaspoon finely chopped coriander (cilantro) stems. To make the filling, combine 80 g (2 3/4 oz) finely diced fresh shiitake mushrooms, 1 teaspoon grated fresh ginger, 6 finely chopped water chestnuts and 1 teaspoon chopped coriander (cilantro) leaves. Stir in 1 teaspoon each of soy sauce, rice wine and sesame oil and 3 teaspoons cornflour. Put a heaped teaspoon of filling in the centre of a wonton wrapper. Moisten the edges with water and gather up the four corners to a peak, encasing the filling. Twist the peak tightly. In a wok or deep-fryer, heat plenty of vegetable oil to 180°C (350°F), or until a cube of bread dropped into the oil browns in 15 seconds. Deep-fry the wontons for about 1 minute, until golden brown. Drain on paper towels and serve with the dipping sauce. Makes 24.

individual pots of baked ricotta and mushrooms

sautéed witlof with olives, anchovies and caperberries .... serves 4

WITLOF (ALSO KNOWN AS CHICORY OR BELGIAN ENDIVE) IS BLANCHED, OR GROWN IN THE DARK, AS DAYLIGHT ENCOURAGES STRONG COLOUR AND A BITTER TASTE, AND THE LOVELY LEAVES LOSE THEIR CRUNCH. THIS METHOD OF PREPARING IT GOES PARTICULARLY WELL WITH TUNA.

pitted kalamata olives	40 g (1½ oz/¼ cup)
anchovy fillets	2
caperberries	5 small
olive oil	1 tablespoon
pale cream or red witlof (chicory/Belgian endive)	2 heads
butter	20 g (³/4 oz)
garlic	1 clove, crushed
chilli flakes	a pinch, optional

Chop the olives and put them in a small bowl. Finely mince the anchovies and add them to the olives. Chop 2 caperberries to the size of baby capers and add to the olives. Add half the olive oil and mix together.

Discard the outer leaves of the witlof and cut in half lengthways. Open out the leaves a little and spoon the olive mixture over and between the leaves. Join the 2 halves together again and tie in place with string.

Heat the remaining oil and the butter in a saucepan over low heat. Add the witlof, garlic and chilli flakes, cover and braise the witlof for 8–10 minutes, turning halfway through. Add a little hot water when necessary to prevent sticking.

To serve, untie the string and arrange the 4 portions of witlof, cut side up, on a serving plate. Spoon over any pan juices. Slice the remaining caperberries in half lengthways and scatter them over the witlof. Serve hot.

Looking like the elongated heart of a baby lettuce, witlof (also known as chicory or Belgian endive) has a fresh bitterness that makes it the perfect accompaniment to intensely flavoured foods like anchovies, olives and strong blue cheeses. Unlike blander vegetables, it is perfectly able to hold its own without being overwhelmed, yet is not so strongly flavoured that it clashes with other ingredients. You can soften the bitterness by slowly braising it in oil, butter or stock. Or strip away whole leaves from the core and fill them with prawns, spiced minced (ground) meat or blue cheese for a platter of neat little canapé cups. Store witlof wrapped in paper or in a paper bag in the refrigerator.

field mushrooms stuffed with gremolata crumbs

serves 4

LARGE FIELD MUSHROOMS ARE WONDERFUL BAKED. LOOK FOR THOSE WITH WHITE UNBLEMISHED SKIN, AND PALE GILLS THAT HAVEN'T DARKENED OR SWEATED. THESE DAYS MUSHROOMS COME TO US IN A VERY CLEAN STATE. IF THEY ARE A LITTLE DIRTY, THEY SHOULD BE WIPED CLEAN WITH A DAMPENED CLOTH, NEVER WASHED.

field mushrooms	4
olive oil	60 ml (2 fl oz/1/4 cup), plus 1/2 teaspoon
streaky bacon	50 g (1 3/4 oz), finely chopped
garlic	3 cloves, crushed
parsley	2 tablespoons chopped
mint	1 tablespoon chopped
lemon zest	1 teaspoon grated
pistachio kernels	25 g (1 oz/1/4 cup) toasted, finely chopped
fresh breadcrumbs	2 tablespoons
ground nutmeg	a pinch
crème fraîche	90 g (3 1/4 oz/1/3 cup)

Preheat the oven to 200°C (400°F/Gas 6). Lightly oil a shallow baking dish. Remove and finely chop the mushroom stalks. Wipe the mushroom caps with a dry paper towel to get rid of any residual grit. Only use a lightly moistened paper towel if the mushrooms have dirt on them. Brush the outside of the caps with olive oil. Arrange in the prepared dish, gills upwards.

Heat 1/2 teaspoon of the olive oil in a small frying pan over high heat. Add the bacon and fry for 1 minute, or until it is crisp and the bacon fat has melted. Add the chopped mushroom stalks and fry for 1 minute. Add the garlic and fry for 15–20 seconds, or until aromatic but not browned.

Remove the pan from the heat and cool for 2–3 minutes. Stir in the parsley, mint, lemon zest, pistachios, breadcrumbs and nutmeg. Season well with salt and freshly ground black pepper.

Scatter the gremolata crumbs into the mushroom caps, covering the gills. Drizzle any remaining olive oil over the top. Bake for 12–15 minutes, or until the crumbs are golden and the mushrooms are soft. Serve hot, with the crème fraîche.

Wipe mushrooms with a damp cloth if they are slightly dirty

Fill the mushroom caps with the gremolata crumbs

balsamic mixed onions .... serves 4

THERE ARE JUST TWO RULES FOR MAKING THIS FINE ACCOMPANIMENT: SELECT ONIONS OF ALL THE SAME SIZE, AND USE THE BEST QUALITY BALSAMIC VINEGAR YOU CAN AFFORD. THIS DISH GOES BEAUTIFULLY WITH BAKED HAM OR ROAST CHICKEN, AND IT ALSO STARS WHEN SERVED AS PART OF AN ANTIPASTO OR A PICNIC SPREAD.

dry white wine	250 ml (9 fl oz/1 cup)
balsamic vinegar	125 ml (4 fl oz/1/2 cup)
olive oil	1 tablespoon
light brown sugar	2 tablespoons
dried bay leaves	2
assorted small onions, such as pearl, red and pickling	1 kg (2 lb 4 oz)
raisins	30 g (1 oz/1/4 cup)

Put the wine, balsamic vinegar, olive oil, sugar and bay leaf in a large saucepan with 2 tablespoons water and bring to the boil. Peel the onions but leave the ends intact; just cut off any roots. Add to the pan and return to the boil.

Add the raisins and simmer gently, tossing occasionally, for 50 minutes, or until the onions are tender and the liquid is thick and syrupy. Transfer to a serving dish and serve at room temperature. Store the onions in a covered container in the refrigerator for up to 2 weeks.

Peel the onions, cutting off roots but leaving ends intact

Bring the onions to the boil in the wine and vinegar mixture

three ways with sweet potato

ALTHOUGH JUST A HUMBLE TUBER, SWEET POTATO RETAINS AN AURA OF THE EXOTIC. THE VARIOUS TYPES MAY HAVE SKINS OF ORANGE, PURPLE OR CREAM, AND FLESH OF WHITE, APRICOT OR ORANGE. CUT THE SURFACE OF SWEET POTATO INTO A DIAMOND PATTERN AND ROAST IT WITH GARLIC AS A PERFECT SIDE FOR ROAST LAMB. ADD A DEEP, CREAMY SWEETNESS TO POLENTA WITH SOFT, MASHED SWEET POTATO, OR GRILL IT WITH BABY LEEKS AND FENNEL FOR A SERIOUSLY YUMMY SIDE DISH.

diamond-cut roast sweet potato and slivered garlic

Peel 2 small orange sweet potatoes (about 14 cm/5½ inches long and 6 cm/2½ inches thick) and halve lengthways. Using a strong, sharp knife, make 1 cm (½ inch) deep cuts in a diamond pattern in the peeled surface, 1.5–2 cm (⅝–¾ inch) apart. Be careful not to cut all the way through. Place, cut side up, on a baking tray. Combine the juice of half an orange with 1 tablespoon olive oil in a small bowl and season well with salt and freshly ground black pepper. Drizzle all over the sweet potato. Scatter 8–10 rosemary sprigs on top and roast in a preheated 190°C (375°F/Gas 5) oven for 20 minutes. Scatter 2 finely sliced garlic cloves over the sweet potato and bake for a further 20–30 minutes, or until tender. Serves 4.

creamy sweet potato polenta

Peel 400 g (14 oz) white sweet potato, cut into chunks and cook in simmering salted water for about 15 minutes, until tender. Drain and mash with 40 g (1½ oz) butter and 60 ml (2 fl oz/¼ cup) cream. Bring 750 ml (26 fl oz/3 cups) water to the boil in a heavy-based saucepan. Add 1 teaspoon salt and slowly stir in 110 g (3¾ oz/¾ cup) instant polenta, breaking up any lumps as you stir. Cook over medium–low heat, stirring often, for 8–10 minutes. Stir in the sweet potato mash and continue cooking and stirring until the polenta is very thick and pulls away from the side of the pan, about 8 minutes. Remove from the heat and season with salt and white pepper, to taste. Serve with a sprinkling of cayenne pepper on top. Serves 4.

chargrilled sweet potato with baby leeks and shaved fennel

Combine 100 ml (3½ fl oz) olive oil, 2 teaspoons chopped mint, 1 crushed garlic clove and plenty of freshly ground black pepper in a bowl. Scrub 1 small narrow (about 400 g/14 oz) orange sweet potato but do not peel. Cut into 1 cm (½ inch) slices, then cut the slices into half-moon shapes. Toss in the oil mixture. Trim 400 g (14 oz/2 bunches) baby leeks and cut into 7–8 cm (2¾–3¼ inches) lengths. Add to the sweet potato and toss to coat. Preheat a barbecue or chargrill pan to medium–high and fry the sweet potato for 4–5 minutes. Add the leeks and continue frying for 3–4 minutes, or until the vegetables are tender. Trim 1 baby fennel bulb, reserving a few green fronds. Slice the fennel very thinly or shave it vertically into whole slices and put it in a bowl with the sweet potato and leeks. Thinly slice 1 small red onion and add, along with 80 g (2¾ oz/scant ½ cup) kalamata olives, 60 ml (2 fl oz/¼ cup) olive oil, 1 tablespoon lemon juice, 1 tablespoon mint leaves and the chopped fennel fronds, to the vegetables. Season with salt and black pepper and toss to combine. Serves 4.

diamond-cut roast sweet potato and slivered garlic

baked fennel with a grana crust................serves 4

THIS IS A WONDERFUL WAY TO PREPARE FENNEL. IT IS A SIMPLE VARIATION ON THE TRADITIONAL GRATINEE, STILL USING CHEESE, MILK AND BUTTER — ALL OF WHICH GO SO WELL WITH THE ANISEED TASTE OF FENNEL — BUT IN MUCH SMALLER AMOUNTS.

fennel	3 bulbs, trimmed
seasoned plain (all-purpose) flour	for dusting
milk	250 ml (9 fl oz/1 cup)
ground nutmeg	1 large pinch
butter	80 g (2 3/4 oz)
grana padano cheese	50 g (1 3/4 oz/1/2 cup) finely grated

Preheat the oven to 180°C (350°F/Gas 4). Grease a large, shallow ovenproof dish. Bring a large saucepan of water to the boil and add 1 teaspoon salt and the whole fennel bulbs. Simmer for 12–15 minutes, or until just tender. Drain and cut each bulb lengthways into quarters, ensuring that each quarter is still attached at the stem.

Dust the fennel with the seasoned flour and lay them in a single layer in the prepared dish. Pour in the milk, sprinkle with nutmeg and dot the butter over the top. Sprinkle with the grana padano. Bake for 30 minutes, or until the cheese top is crusty, the fennel is fork tender and the milk forms a little sauce.

Of the two types of fennel, one is grown for its feathery fronds, the other (also known as Florence fennel or finocchio) for its thick stems and bulbous base. The seeds of both types have culinary uses. All parts taste of aniseed. The fresh flavour and crisp texture of the raw bulbs make them delicious in salad. Or, for a softer texture and sweeter flavour, the bulbs can be braised or roasted whole; if halved or quartered, they will caramelize beautifully. The gentle flavour of the pretty fronds can subtly spice up fish and vegetable dishes. Fennel is best used straight after harvesting; luckily, it is perfectly suited to domestic cultivation. To store fennel, wrap in a damp tea towel and put it in the vegetable crisper of the fridge.

onions

peeling

Cutting an onion releases a compound that irritates the eyes. The more cut surfaces that are exposed to air, the more volatile the compound becomes. Try one of these steps to overcome the discomfort:

Soak the onions in water for 30 minutes before peeling
Peel under an open window or exhaust fan
Chill the onions beforehand
Breathe with your mouth open

To peel pickling or pearl onions, or any which are to be used whole or in wedges, do not trim them. Keeping the root intact will prevent the layers from falling apart during cooking, while retaining the top gives an attractive shape. Peel off the outer leaves one or two at a time from the top down towards the root.

slicing

After peeling the onion, take a little slice off its middle and stand the onion on this to stabilize it. Starting at one end, slice into rings until you are close to the middle, then move to the other end and slice back towards the middle. This will give you the steadiest hold for the longest time.

To slice Asian style, halve the onion from top to bottom and place the cut surface on the chopping board. Starting at one side, slice lengthways into desired widths.

dicing

Cut the peeled onion in half from top to bottom. Lay one half, cut surface down, on the chopping board with the root end away from you. Cut lengthways into slices, keeping the slices attached at the root. Now slice horizontally back towards the root, being careful not to cut through it. Next, starting at the far end and working towards the root, slice down through the previous cuts, giving diced pieces. Discard the root.

sweet spinach pie .... serves 6

THIS SURPRISING BUT DELICIOUS COMBINATION IS FROM PROVENCE, IN FRANCE. HAVING LOW-GROWING FOLIAGE, SPINACH NEEDS A THOROUGH WASHING TO GET RID OF SOIL AND BUGS. IT IS IDEALLY COOKED BRIEFLY AND WITHOUT ADDED WATER, JUST THAT WHICH REMAINS CLINGING TO THE LEAVES AFTER RINSING.

pastry

plain (all-purpose) flour	250 g (9 oz/2 cups)
caster (superfine) sugar	1 teaspoon
butter	125 g (4 1/2 oz), chilled and cubed
egg yolk	1

filling

English spinach leaves	350 g (12 oz), stemmed and rinsed
milk	300 ml (10 1/2 fl oz)
vanilla bean	1, split
raw caster (superfine) sugar	60 g (2 1/4 oz/ 1/4 cup)
plain (all-purpose) flour	30 g (1 oz/ 1/4 cup)
egg yolks	2
orange zest	2 tablespoons finely grated
currants	2 tablespoons, optional
candied orange slices	4, to garnish (optional)
egg	1, beaten
pine nuts	2 tablespoons
thick (double/heavy) cream	to serve

To make the pastry, put the flour, sugar, 1/4 teaspoon salt and the butter in a food processor. Pulse until fine and crumbly. Add the egg yolk, process to combine, then add 1 teaspoon of water at a time and pulse just until the dough clumps into a ball. Knead lightly to a smooth ball. Press into a disc, cover with plastic wrap and chill for 30 minutes.

To make the filling, put the spinach in a large saucepan with a pinch of salt. Cover and cook over low heat for 4–5 minutes, or until wilted, turning the leaves over once or twice. Drain.

Put the milk, vanilla bean and sugar in a medium heavy-based saucepan and bring slowly to the boil. Remove from the heat and cool for 10 minutes, then discard the vanilla bean. Mix the flour and egg yolks together in a medium bowl. Stir in the warm milk and whisk until smooth. Return the mixture to the saucepan, add the orange zest and bring to the boil over low heat, stirring constantly. Remove from the heat and set aside to cool.

Preheat the oven to 190°C (375°F/Gas 5). Grease a 20 cm (8 inch) smooth-sided tart or pie tin and line with 2 strips of foil. Roll out the pastry between 2 sheets of baking paper to 2–3 mm (1/16 inch) thick and use to line the prepared tin. Reserve any trimmings. Line the pastry with crumpled baking paper and fill with baking weights or dried beans. Bake blind for 15 minutes. Remove the weights and paper and bake for a further 8 minutes, or until light golden brown. Cool for 5 minutes. Put a baking tray on the centre shelf of the oven.

Stir the spinach and currants into the cooled custard, then spoon into the pastry case. Place an orange slice in the centre. Halve the remainder and arrange around the edge. Roll out the pastry trimmings and cut six strips. Use to make a spoke pattern between the orange slices. Brush the entire surface with beaten egg, then scatter with the pine nuts. Put on the tray in the oven and bake for 20–25 minutes, or until the pie is golden and the filling is set. Serve hot or warm, with thick (double/heavy) cream.

Whisk together the egg mixture and warm milk to form a custard

Cross two foil strips to act as handles when removing the pie

white sweet potato loaf............ makes one 20 x 8 cm (8 x 3¹/₄ inch) loaf

ALTHOUGH UNRELATED TO THEIR NAMESAKE, SWEET POTATOES, LIKE POTATOES, ARE TUBERS AND ARE A GOOD SOURCE OF CARBOHYDRATES AND VITAMINS. THE FLESH OF THE SWEET POTATO DISCOLOURS WHEN EXPOSED TO AIR, SO PLACE THE PIECES IN COLD WATER AS SOON AS THEY'RE PEELED AND CUT.

white sweet potato	175–200 g (6–7 oz)
butter	125 g (4¹/₂ oz), at room temperature
caster (superfine) sugar	125 g (4¹/₂ oz/¹/₂ cup)
eggs	2
self-raising flour	125 g (4¹/₂ oz/1 cup), sifted
milk	60 ml (2 fl oz/¹/₄ cup)
natural vanilla flavouring	1 teaspoon
candied or preserved orange rind	35 g (1¹/₄ oz), chopped
currants	50 g (1³/₄ oz/¹/₃ cup)
icing (confectioners') sugar	to serve

Peel the sweet potato and cut it into chunks. Put it in a saucepan and cover with cold water. Bring to the boil, then reduce the heat and simmer for about 15 minutes, until tender, then drain. Set aside to cool for 15 minutes. Mash the sweet potato until smooth with a potato masher or a ricer (do not use a food processor). You will need 150 g (5¹/₂ oz/²/₃ cup) mashed sweet potato. Cover and refrigerate until cold.

Preheat the oven to 180°C (350°F/Gas 4). Grease and line a 20 x 8 cm (8 x 3¹/₄ inch) loaf tin. Cream the butter and sugar with an electric mixer on medium–high speed for 3 minutes. Add the eggs, one at a time, beating well after each addition. Stir in the cold mashed sweet potato. With a wooden spoon, stir in the flour alternately with the milk and beat lightly until smooth. Stir in the vanilla, orange rind and currants.

Spread the mixture in the prepared tin and bake for 40–45 minutes, or until a skewer inserted in the centre comes out clean. Set aside for 10 minutes before turning out onto a wire rack to cool. Dust with icing sugar to serve. Cut into slices and serve for afternoon tea, or take on a picnic. Store for up to 7 days in an airtight container in the refrigerator.

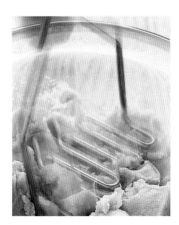

Mash the cooked sweet potato until smooth, then allow to cool

Stir the vanilla, orange rind and currants into the batter

Leave in the tin for 10 minutes, then turn out onto a wire rack

Winter is a time to cocoon yourself and rediscover the kitchen as the true heart of your home. As the weather grows cold and the evenings draw in, the gently domestic becomes incredibly appealing. Unlike summer, when fresh is king and fast is the order of the day, winter is about seeking comfort in slow, considered food. Pottering in the kitchen becomes a pleasurable way of whiling away a gloomy afternoon, and tackling a complicated recipe is a challenge to relish.

It is so easy to think of winter as a barren time, but one look at the bounty of winter's harvest should dispel that misconception. This is the season in which root vegetables come into their own. Potatoes, parsnips, turnips and carrots are straight from the ground, their skins still dusted with soil. Silverbeet, cabbage and baby brussels sprouts are sweet, crisp and bursting with goodness. Winter squash and jerusalem artichokes are full of flavour, and shallots are the perfect way to add a sweet, piquant edge to the slow-cooked classics of winter fare.

Celebrating the unique rhythm of each season is as much about method as it is about menu. The cosy warmth of a busy oven takes the edge off a chilly day. Bubbling pots of hearty food permeate the house with tempting aromas, whetting appetites and teasing taste buds. Winter is the time when nostalgia and reality come together in the steamy haze of a bustling kitchen.

Slow cooking heightens both the flavour of the food and the anticipation of the diner. Think of the way that a Sunday roast fills the house with mouth-watering aromas for hours before it finally graces the table. Roasting, braising and caramelizing bring out the natural sweetness of vegetables, intensifying their flavour. Consider, also, that method applied with forethought can turn a humble vegetable into a masterpiece. Experiment with an unfamiliar ingredient, or try a new way with an old favourite.

Vegetables may not always be the star of the show, but that's no reason for them not to shine. Winter is the season where the desire for a large, juicy piece of meat can verge on a craving, but none of this lessens the role that vegetables play in a meal. A winter table without an array of perfectly cooked seasonal vegetables is essentially a table bereft, devoid of the life-enhancing vitality of nature's bounty. As winter weather draws you home, take comfort in the face of cold, dark days with honest fare lovingly cooked. Revel in this short respite from the daily diet's health imperatives and indulge in the guilt-free luxury of the winter table.

parsnip and pecan fritters . . . . serves 4

THE DISTINCTIVE FLAVOUR OF PARSNIPS IS RELIANT ON THE ICY SNAP OF WINTER. THEY CONVERT STARCH INTO SUGAR AFTER SITTING IN THE COLD GROUND FOR A NUMBER OF WEEKS, AND THE FLESH BECOMES SWEETER. OLD OR LARGE SPECIMENS MAY NEED TO HAVE THEIR TOUGH CORE REMOVED BEFORE COOKING.

dipping sauce

sour cream	200 g (7 oz/heaped $^3/_4$ cup)
chives	1 tablespoon finely chopped
lemon juice	1 teaspoon
sweet chilli sauce	2 tablespoons
Tabasco sauce	3–4 drops
parsnips	375 g (13 oz)
egg	1
plain (all-purpose) flour	30 g (1 oz/$^1/_4$ cup)
parsley	1 tablespoon chopped
butter	50 g (1$^3/_4$ oz), melted
milk	60 ml (2 fl oz/$^1/_4$ cup)
pecans	60 g (2$^1/_4$ oz/$^2/_3$ cup), coarsely chopped
cayenne pepper	a large pinch
oil	250 ml (9 fl oz/1 cup)

To make the dipping sauce, combine the sour cream, chives, lemon juice, sweet chilli sauce and Tabasco sauce, to taste, in a serving bowl.

Peel the parsnips, cut them into chunks and immediately place in a saucepan of water. Bring to the boil. Add $^1/_2$ teaspoon salt, reduce the heat and simmer for 15–20 minutes, or until tender, then drain. Purée the parsnip with a potato ricer or mouli, discarding any tough bits. Transfer to a bowl and mix with the egg, flour, parsley, butter, milk, pecans and cayenne pepper. Season with salt, to taste.

Heat the oil in a non-stick frying pan over medium heat. Drop in 1$^1/_2$ tablespoons of mixture at a time and flatten slightly with the back of a spoon. Fry, turning once, for 15–20 seconds, or until golden. Remove with a slotted spoon and drain on paper towels. Serve hot, accompanied by the dipping sauce.

Purée the parsnip with a potato ricer or mouli

Fry flattened spoonfuls of the mixture in hot oil until golden

silverbeet ravioli with browned butter

BUY NEW-SEASON SILVERBEET (SWISS CHARD) AT THE BEGINNING OF WINTER FOR YOUNG AND TENDER LEAVES. THE FLAVOUR IS SWEET AND DELICATE AND THE COLOUR BRIGHT. IT IS IMPORTANT TO USE A DRY RICOTTA FOR THE FILLING, SO BUY IT OFF THE BLOCK FROM A DELICATESSEN IN PREFERENCE TO PRE-PACKED TUBS.

filling

silverbeet (Swiss chard)	1.25 kg (2 lb 12 oz/1 large bunch)
ricotta cheese	175 g (6 oz/³⁄4 cup)
spring onions (scallions)	4, white part only, finely chopped
egg yolk	1
pecorino pepato cheese	30 g (1 oz/¹⁄4 cup) finely grated
ground nutmeg	¹⁄2 teaspoon
butter	125 g (4¹⁄2 oz)
oil	1 tablespoon
small basil leaves	1 small handful
square wonton wrappers	32
egg	1, lightly beaten

To make the filling, strip the silverbeet leaves off the stalks, discarding the stalks. You should have about 350 g (12 oz) of leaves. Rinse under cold water and shake off the excess. Put the leaves in a large saucepan with a large pinch of salt. Cover and cook over medium heat for 5–6 minutes, or until wilted and tender. Turn the silverbeet over once or twice to distribute the heat. While the silverbeet is still warm, chop the leaves medium–fine (do not use a food processor). Put in a dry tea towel and wring out the residual water. Put the silverbeet in a bowl and add the ricotta, spring onion, egg yolk, pecorino and nutmeg and season well with salt and pepper.

Melt the butter in a small saucepan over low heat and cook for 3–4 minutes, or until golden. Remove from the heat and set aside. Heat the oil in a small frying pan over medium heat and fry the basil for 15–20 seconds, or until bright and crisp. Drain on paper towels.

Spread 6–8 wonton wrappers on a clean work surface. Brush around the edges with the beaten egg. Spoon a tablespoon of filling on the centre of each wrapper. Cover with another wrapper and press the edges together tightly to seal. Repeat with the remaining wrappers and filling.

Strain the butter through a fine sieve into a clean saucepan and warm over very low heat. Bring a large saucepan of water to the boil. Add 1 tablespoon of salt and cook the ravioli, in batches, for 1–1¹⁄2 minutes, or until al dente. Remove with a slotted spoon and transfer to a warm bowl.

Divide the ravioli among 4 serving dishes. Spoon some butter over the ravioli and scatter the basil on top. Serve immediately.

Put the cooked spinach in a tea towel and wring out excess water

Sandwich a tablespoon of filling between two wonton wrappers

french shallot, bacon and cheddar breakfast muffins
.... makes 6 large muffins

SERVED WARM WITH LASHINGS OF BUTTER, THESE MUFFINS ARE JUST THE THING FOR COLD WEEKEND MORNINGS. THEY CAN BE MADE THE DAY BEFORE, STORED IN AN AIRTIGHT CONTAINER AND REHEATED WHEN NEEDED. FRENCH SHALLOTS ARE PREFERABLE, BUT ASIAN CAN BE USED TOO.

oil	60 ml (2 fl oz/1/4 cup), plus 2 teaspoons
French shallots	5
bacon	2 slices, finely chopped
plain (all-purpose) flour	250 g (9 oz/2 cups)
baking powder	1 tablespoon
raw caster (superfine) sugar	1 tablespoon
dry mustard	1 teaspoon
mature cheddar cheese	140 g (5 oz/scant 1 1/4 cups) shredded
milk	185 ml (6 fl oz/3/4 cup)
egg	1
sweet paprika	to serve

Preheat the oven to 200°C (400°F/Gas 6). Grease a 6-hole giant muffin tin.

Finely slice 1 of the shallots into rings. Finely chop the remaining 4 shallots. Heat 2 teaspoons of the oil in a small non-stick frying pan over low heat. Add the sliced shallot and fry, without browning, for 3 minutes. Remove from the pan and drain on paper towels. Increase the heat to medium–low and add the chopped shallots and bacon to the pan. Fry for about 5 minutes, until the shallots are soft. Drain on paper towels.

Sift the flour, baking powder, sugar, mustard and 1/2 teaspoon salt into a large bowl. Add 90 g (3 1/4 oz/3/4 cup) of the cheddar and the bacon mixture and stir through. Combine the milk, egg and remaining oil in a pitcher. Pour into the bowl and fold gently until combined. Do not beat; the batter should be lumpy.

Divide the batter among the muffin holes. Top each with a few of the fried shallot rings and some of the remaining shredded cheddar. Bake for 20–25 minutes, or until the muffins are risen and golden and a fine skewer inserted into the centre of a muffin comes out clean. Cool in the tin for 5 minutes before turning out. Sprinkle a little paprika on top to serve.

Fry the bacon and chopped shallots until the shallots are soft

Fold the milk, egg and remaining oil through the flour mixture

Divide the batter among the muffin holes, then scatter with cheese

baked swedes with ricotta, blue cheese and sage.............................serves 4

SWEDES, OR RUTABAGA, RESEMBLE TURNIPS, BUT HAVE A MORE MELLOW FLAVOUR AND A CREAMIER TEXTURE. THEY GO WELL WITH OTHER VEGETABLES, AND THEY ROAST AND BAKE BEAUTIFULLY. FOR THIS RECIPE, USE BULK RICOTTA FROM THE DELI COUNTER RATHER THAN THAT IN PRE-PACKED TUBS, WHICH IS WETTER AND GRAINIER.

swedes (rutabaga)	4 medium, scrubbed
olive oil	1½ tablespoons
butter	2 tablespoons
creamy blue vein cheese	55 g (2 oz), crumbled
ricotta cheese	125 g (½ cup)
sage	12 leaves
garlic	1 clove, crushed

Preheat the oven to 180°C (350°F/Gas 4). Rub the swedes with one-third of the oil. Place each in the centre of a 30 cm (12 inch) square of foil, season lightly with salt and pepper and dot with the butter. Fold up the foil to enclose the swedes. Arrange, root down, in a small baking dish and bake until tender, about 1 hour.

Mix the blue cheese and ricotta together in a small saucepan and heat over a low heat until soft and flowing. Keep warm. Heat the remaining olive oil in a small frying pan until hot. Fry the sage leaves until crisp, 8–10 seconds. Drain on paper towels.

Add the garlic to the pan, reduce the heat to low and fry until just beginning to colour, 12–15 seconds. Transfer to the cheese mixture and add 4 of the sage leaves. Season to taste with salt and freshly ground black pepper and stir to combine.

Remove the foil from the swedes and cut them diagonally into 2–3 cm (3/4–1¼ inch) slices. Reassemble to serve, with the sauce spooned over the top. Top with the remaining sage leaves.

The closest many of us come to a swede is via the packs of soup vegetables that are available from supermarkets throughout the winter months. Swedes are like a finer, sweeter turnip and are best suited to soups, stews and mashing. They are not a true root vegetable, but a vegetable with a swollen base at the stem. Choose unblemished specimens with a purplish top and fresh green stalk for the finest flavour. Swedes can be stored in the fridge for up to ten days, though they will soften and their flavour strengthen. Should you find the flavour too strong, simply blanch them for 10 minutes, then discard the cooking water and resume cooking in fresh water.

warm salad of jerusalem artichoke, radicchio and pastrami......... serves 4

TO STOP THEM GOING BROWN, JERUSALEM ARTICHOKES SHOULD BE PUT IN ACIDULATED WATER ONCE CUT, AND ALWAYS COOKED IN A NON-REACTIVE PAN. THESE TUBERS CAN INDUCE FLATULENCE IN SOME PEOPLE; THIS CAN BE COUNTERED WITH ASAFOETIDA, A SPICE AVAILABLE FROM INDIAN AND MIDDLE EASTERN STORES.

jerusalem artichokes	500 g (1 lb 2 oz)
lemon	juice of 1/2
asafoetida	a pinch
treviso radicchio	1
golden walnut pieces	40 g (1 1/2 oz/1/3 cup)
walnut oil	60 ml (2 fl oz/1/4 cup)
orange	1 small, zested and juiced
parsley	1 tablespoon shredded
pastrami	100 g (3 1/2 oz) slices, halved

Peel the artichokes. Cut any large ones to give pieces of roughly the same size. Put the artichokes in a non-reactive saucepan of boiling salted water with the lemon juice and asafoetida. Simmer for 12 minutes, or until tender, then drain. When cool, slice the artichokes on the diagonal.

Preheat the grill (broiler) to hot. Trim off any coarse outer leaves from the radicchio and quarter it lengthways. Put the radicchio, cut side up, in a medium shallow heatproof dish, scatter the walnuts on top and drizzle with half the oil. Grill (broil) for 1–2 minutes, or until the leaves start to pucker and the edges brown. Remove from the heat and set aside to cool for 2–3 minutes.

Cut off the radicchio stems and return the leaves to the dish. Add the artichokes, orange juice and parsley and season with salt and freshly ground black pepper, to taste. Toss lightly. Scrunch the pastrami pieces into loose balls and arrange them among the artichokes. Drizzle with the remaining walnut oil and return to the grill. Grill for 1–2 minutes, or until just beginning to brown. Top with the orange zest and serve immediately.

Jerusalem artichokes look more like a knobbly potato than their green-petaled namesake, to which they are not related. The trick to cooking with jerusalem artichokes is to treat them as you would a potato. They are delicious steamed, roasted, baked or mashed with lashings of butter. Although easy to cook, they require a little time and effort in the preparation. Peeling their knobbly skin with a regular vegetable peeler can be time-consuming and irritating. You may want to sacrifice a little of the flesh and do it the easy way by taking a decent-sized knife and treating the jerusalem artichoke as though it were a pineapple – just take off the top and slice down around the curve for a perfectly peeled specimen.

three ways with carrots

CARROTS ARE A PRECIOUS GIFT — A WINTER VEGETABLE THAT CAN BE EATEN WITH RELISH WHETHER RAW OR COOKED. THIS SEASON'S HARVEST IS THE LEANEST AND THE WINTER COOK NEEDS TO BE INVENTIVE. THE SOFTNESS OF ROASTED CARROTS GOES WELL WITH THE SMOKY SWEETNESS OF GARLIC. MAKE THE MOST OF THEIR NATURAL SWEETNESS BY PAIRING CARROTS WITH ORANGES AND OLIVES IN A SPICY SALAD. FOR A ZESTY WINTER SIDE DISH TO LIFT YOUR SPIRITS, JUST STIR-FRY THE CARROTS WITH LASHINGS OF TASTY GINGER AND MINT.

roasted carrots with olive oil and garlic

Scrub 750 g (1 lb 10 oz) carrots and cut them lengthways into quarters. Put the carrots on a baking tray with 1 tablespoon olive oil and a large pinch of salt. Toss to coat, and spread in a single layer. Roast in a preheated 220°C (425°F/Gas 7) oven for 30 minutes. Add 3 unpeeled garlic cloves and 2 sliced garlic cloves and roast for a further 10 minutes, or until the carrots are golden and tender. Squeeze the garlic from the unpeeled cloves into a small bowl and mash to a paste. Add 2 tablespoons mascarpone cheese, 2 teaspoons each of extra virgin olive oil and lime juice, 1/4 teaspoon grated lime zest, and salt and pepper, to taste. Serve the carrots and sliced garlic with the dressing spooned over the top. Serves 4.

moroccan salad with orange and black olives

Peel 600 g (1 lb 5 oz) baby (Dutch) carrots and trim their stalks, leaving about 2 cm (3/4 inch). Bring a large saucepan of water to the boil and add 1/2 teaspoon salt and the carrots. Simmer until the carrots are just tender, then drain and transfer to a shallow dish. Thinly slice 1 small red onion into rings and add to the carrots, along with 60 g (21/4 oz/1/3 cup) black olives. Put 1 crushed garlic clove, 2 tablespoons each of olive oil and orange juice, 1 teaspoon grated orange zest, a scant 1/2 teaspoon paprika, 1/4 teaspoon each of chilli flakes and ground cumin, and a pinch of sugar in a small bowl and whisk to combine. Pour over the carrots and toss gently to coat. Serve warm or at room temperature. Serves 4.

stir-fried carrots with ginger and mint

Peel 600 g (1 lb 5 oz) carrots and cut on the diagonal into 5 mm (1/4 inch) thick slices. Heat 30 g (1 oz) butter in a frying pan over medium heat. Add 1 teaspoon grated palm sugar, 1 scant teaspoon grated fresh ginger and the carrots. Fry, stirring constantly, for 1 minute, without browning. Add 60 ml (2 fl oz/1/4 cup) each of mango juice and hot water, increase the heat and boil for 3–4 minutes, or until most of the liquid has evaporated. Add 1 small handful torn mint and season lightly with salt and white pepper. Serves 4.

bavarian potato soup with fresh horseradish cream ....serves 4

POTATO SOUP IS WARMING, FILLING AND TOTALLY COMFORTING. BUT WHILE POTATOES CAN BE BOUGHT ALL YEAR, FRESH HORSERADISH APPEARS FOR JUST A SHORT PERIOD EARLY IN WINTER. TAKE ADVANTAGE OF THIS AND MAKE YOUR OWN HORSERADISH CREAM; SMOOTH AND CREAMY, IT SURPASSES THE BOUGHT PRODUCT.

horseradish cream

thick (double/heavy) cream	80 ml (2½ fl oz/⅓ cup)
lemon juice	1 teaspoon
fresh horseradish	1 small
caster (superfine) sugar	a small pinch
butter	60 g (2¼ oz/¼ cup)
leek	1, white part only, thinly sliced
waxy potatoes, preferably kipfler	1 kg (2 lb 4 oz), peeled and coarsely diced
celeriac	½ small, peeled and coarsely diced
carrot	1, scrubbed and diced
onion	1, diced
garlic	1 clove, coarsely chopped
thyme	¼ teaspoon, plus 4 sprigs
cream	250 ml (9 fl oz/1 cup)
ground nutmeg	to taste
speck	100 g (3½ oz) piece
olive oil	2 teaspoons
stale white bread	4 thick slices

To make the horseradish cream, combine the cream and lemon juice in a small bowl. Thinly peel the horseradish and grate it finely to give 1 tablespoon. Immediately stir it through the cream mixture. Add the sugar and a small pinch of salt. The acid from the lemon juice will react with the horseradish and thicken the cream mixture.

Heat the butter in a large heavy-based saucepan over low heat. Add the leek and fry for 4–5 minutes, or until softened. Remove from the pan. Add the potato, celeriac, carrot, onion, garlic and thyme to the pan and fry for 2 minutes. Add cold water to cover and bring to the boil, then reduce the heat and simmer slowly for 45 minutes.

Transfer half the contents of the pan to a food processor and blend until smooth. Return to the saucepan and add the cream, leek and nutmeg, to taste. Simmer for 5 minutes. Season well with salt and freshly ground black pepper.

Cut the speck into 1 cm (½ inch) cubes. Heat the oil in a frying pan over medium heat and fry the speck for 4–5 minutes, or until lightly browned. Remove from the pan and drain on paper towels. Cut the crusts off the bread and cut it into 1 cm (½ inch) cubes. Add to the pan and cook for 4–5 minutes, or until brown. Drain on paper towels.

Spoon the soup into bowls and scatter each serving with croutons, speck and a sprig of thyme. Serve the horseradish cream separately for diners to stir into their bowls, to taste.

Note: Ungrated peeled fresh horseradish can be kept for up to 5 days if covered with vinegar and refrigerated.

Finely grate the horseradish to give 1 tablespoon

Fry the croutons for 4–5 minutes, or until lightly browned

brussels sprouts with pancetta .... serves 4

THE REPUTATION OF BRUSSELS SPROUTS IS NOT GOOD, BUT WHEN YOUNG, THEY ARE FLAVOURFUL AND CRISP, AND MAKE A GOOD ACCOMPANIMENT TO COLD-WEATHER ROASTS AND STEWS. THIS DISH GOES PARTICULARLY WELL WITH FRIED OR GRILLED PORK SAUSAGES.

pancetta	100 g (3½ oz) thinly sliced
French shallots	4
butter	20 g (¾ oz)
olive oil	1 tablespoon
garlic	1 clove, crushed
young brussels sprouts	500 g (1 lb 2 oz), trimmed and thickly sliced

Preheat the grill (broiler) to hot. Spread the pancetta on a baking sheet or on a grill rack lined with foil and put the sheet or rack 8–10 cm (3¼–4 inches) under the heat source. Grill (broil) for 45–60 seconds, or until crisp. Set aside to cool.

Peel the shallots and cut them into thick rings. Heat the butter and oil in a large frying pan over medium heat. Add the shallots and garlic and fry for 3–4 minutes, or until just starting to brown. Add the brussels sprouts and season with freshly ground black pepper. Fry, stirring often, for 4–5 minutes, or until partly golden and crisp. Turn off the heat, cover and set aside for 5 minutes.

Break the pancetta into large shards. Add to the brussels sprouts and toss lightly; some will break up into smaller pieces. Divide among 4 plates and serve immediately.

Cut the brussels sprouts into thick slices

Break the grilled pancetta into large shards

radicchio and veal rolls

THE SWEETNESS OF BUTTER AND BALSAMIC VINEGAR OFFSETS THE SHARPNESS OF THE TREVISO RADICCHIO. THIS IS A GREAT LAST-MINUTE OPTION FOR A SPECIAL DINNER. USE THE BEST-QUALITY BALSAMIC VINEGAR YOU CAN FIND; IT IS WORTH THE EXTRA EXPENSE.

treviso radicchio	2
olive oil	2 tablespoons
balsamic vinegar	2 tablespoons
veal	4 thin slices scaloppine, each about 100 g (3½ oz)
parmesan cheese	40 g (1½ oz) freshly grated
butter	3 tablespoons

Trim the outer leaves from the radicchio and cut each head in half lengthways. Heat the oil in a large non-stick pan and fry the radicchio over a medium heat until lightly browned all over, 3–4 minutes. Season with salt and freshly ground black pepper and add 2 teaspoons of balsamic vinegar. Turn to coat, then remove from the pan.

Season the veal on both sides with salt and pepper and sprinkle parmesan cheese over one side. With the parmesan on the inside, wrap a slice of veal around the middle of each radicchio half, securing it in place with a toothpick.

Wipe the pan out with a paper towel. Melt the butter in the pan and add the veal rolls. Brown quickly over medium–high heat, turning often. Add the remaining balsamic vinegar, cook for 5–6 seconds and remove from the heat. Turn the rolls to coat. Serve with the pan juices spooned over the top, accompanied by your favourite mash.

With its beautiful deep red colour and mildly bitter taste, treviso radicchio is a wonderfully simple way to spice up a basic salad. This vegetable resembles a red lettuce with elongated leaves. Its heart looks like a red Belgian endive, but the leaves are glossier. They can be shredded and used in pastas and stews, but it is when stirred through a risotto that they really come into their own. All types of radicchio can be stored in the fridge for several days and keep best wrapped in a damp tea towel. As with all leafy vegetables, it is best not to wash radicchio before storing, but to wait until you are ready to use it. There are two other types of radicchio; these and treviso radicchio are all known as Italian chicory.

three ways with broccoli

CHILDHOOD EXHORTATIONS TO 'EAT UP YOUR BROCCOLI' HAVE LANDED THIS VEGETABLE WITH AN UNDESERVED REPUTATION. NOT JUST EXTREMELY GOOD FOR YOU, BROCCOLI IS ALSO DELICIOUS AND, WHEN PREPARED PROPERLY, SHOULD TEMPT EVEN THE MOST RELUCTANT EATER. SHALLOTS AND CHESTNUTS BRING A NUTTY EDGE TO SIMPLY STEAMED BROCCOLI. MIX FINELY CHOPPED BROCCOLI WITH CREAMY RICOTTA FOR A LIGHT AND FLUFFY DISH OF YUMMY GOODNESS, OR UP THE BREAKFAST ANTE WITH SCRAMBLED EGGS AND BROCCOLI.

broccoli, shallots and chestnuts

Boil 200 g (7 oz/3^1/$_3$ cups) small broccoli florets in a large pan of boiling salted water for 4 minutes. Remove with a slotted spoon. Peel and clean 150 g (5^1/$_2$ oz) fresh chestnuts, or use 100 g (3^1/$_2$ oz) frozen peeled chestnuts. Add to the boiling water and cook for 12–15 minutes, or until tender (the chestnuts may break up). Drain the chestnuts. Heat 60 ml (2 fl oz/^{1}/$_4$ cup) oil in a large frying pan over high heat. Fry 2 thin slices pancetta for about 1 minute, until crisp. Drain on paper towels. Wipe out the pan and heat 2 teaspoons olive oil over low heat. Add 3 quartered, peeled French shallots and 1 crushed garlic clove. Fry for 5 minutes, or until softened. Stir in the chestnuts and cook for 2 minutes. Add the broccoli and 1 teaspoon hazelnut oil and cook until heated through. Break the pancetta into shards and add to the pan along with some freshly ground black pepper. Serves 4.

broccoli and ricotta souffle

Cook 60 g (2^1/$_4$ oz/1 cup) small broccoli florets in boiling salted water for 4 minutes, then drain. Heat 2 tablespoons olive oil and 40 g (1^1/$_2$ oz) butter in a frying pan over medium heat. Fry 1 finely chopped onion for 6 minutes, or until soft. Transfer to a large bowl and add the broccoli, 450 g (1 lb) ricotta cheese, 55 g (2 oz/^{1}/$_2$ cup) grated parmesan cheese, 3 lightly beaten eggs, a pinch each of nutmeg and cayenne pepper, and salt and pepper, to taste. Mix well. Whisk 4 egg whites with a pinch each of salt and cream of tartar in a bowl until stiff peaks form. Gently fold one-third of the egg white into the broccoli mixture, then lightly incorporate the remainder. Grease a 1 litre (35 fl oz/4 cup) soufflé dish and sprinkle with 25 g (1 oz/^{1}/$_4$ cup) dry breadcrumbs. Turn the dish to coat the edges with the breadcrumbs. Upturn the dish to discard any that do not stick. Spoon the broccoli mixture into the dish and bake in a preheated 190°C (375°F/Gas 5) oven for 35–40 minutes, or until puffed and golden brown. Serves 4.

broccoli with scrambled eggs

Cook 400 g (14 oz/6^2/$_3$ cups) broccoli florets with some tender stems attached in boiling salted water for 5–8 minues, or until just tender, then drain. Heat 60 ml (2 fl oz/^{1}/$_4$ cup) light olive oil in a frying pan over medium heat. Fry 1 peeled garlic clove and 1 chopped, seeded red bird's eye chilli for 2 minutes. Add the broccoli and toss to coat. Heat for 1 minute, shaking the pan to prevent sticking. Discard the garlic. Push the broccoli to one side of the pan. Combine 2 eggs and 2 tablespoons grated pecorino cheese and season lightly with salt and freshly ground black pepper. Add to the pan and stir with a fork until creamy, but not yet set. Incorporate the broccoli and toss lightly. Serve immediately. Serves 4.

stifatho ....serves 4

BABY ONIONS ARE THE BASIS OF THIS TRADITIONAL BEEF DISH FROM GREECE, AND IT IS SAID THAT THE SIGN OF A GOOD COOK IS ONIONS THAT ARE KEPT WHOLE, BUT COOKED LONG ENOUGH TO BE TENDER AND IMPART THEIR FLAVOUR TO THE BEEF.

stewing steak	1 kg (2 lb 4 oz), trimmed
olive oil	80 ml (2 1/2 fl oz/1/3 cup)
brown onion	1 large, finely chopped
garlic	2 cloves, thinly sliced
ground allspice (pimento)	1/4 teaspoon
ground cumin	1/2 teaspoon
tomato paste (concentrated purée)	60 g (2 1/4 oz/1/4 cup)
dry red wine	170 ml (5 1/2 fl oz/2/3 cup)
red wine vinegar	2 tablespoons
bay leaf	1, torn in half
cinnamon stick	1, broken in half
beef stock	250 ml (9 fl oz/1 cup)
baby onions	800 g (1 lb 12 oz)
sultanas (golden raisins)	2 tablespoons

Preheat the oven to 160°C (315°F/Gas 2–3). Cut the beef into 2 cm (3/4 inch) thick slices, then into 3 cm (1 1/4 inch) cubes. Heat half the olive oil in a large flameproof casserole dish over high heat. Fry the beef, in batches, for 7–8 minutes, or until browned, then transfer to a bowl.

Add the remaining oil, chopped onion and garlic to the casserole, reduce the heat to low and fry for 5–6 minutes, or until soft. Add the allspice and cumin and cook for 1 minute. Return the beef to the casserole, increase the heat and stir well to coat with the spices. Add the tomato paste, wine and vinegar and cook for 1 minute. Add the bay leaf, cinnamon stick, stock and enough hot water to cover the beef. Bring to the boil, then cover and transfer to the oven. Bake for 1 hour.

Remove the loose outer skin of the onions but do not peel them entirely or top and tail them. Cut a cross in the root. Bring a large saucepan of water to the boil and add the onions. Boil for 1 minute, then drain. The inner skins will have been loosened and will peel off easily.

Add the baby onions to the casserole, along with the sultanas, and toss lightly. If necessary, top up with hot water to keep the contents just covered. Bake for a further 1 hour, or until the meat and onions are tender but not breaking up. Discard the bay leaf and pieces of cinnamon stick before serving.

Fry the beef, in batches, until well browned

Remove the loose outer skins of the onions

cavolo nero with ribollita .... serves 6-8

A WHOLESOME ITALIAN MAIN-MEAL SOUP, RIBOLLITA MEANS REBOILED. THE NAME REFERS TO A LARGE POT BEING MADE IN ADVANCE, WITH SERVINGS REBOILED AS NEEDED. THE DARK GREEN LEAVES OF CAVOLO NERO ARE THE BACKBONE OF RIBOLLITA, BUT KALE OR SAVOY CABBAGE MAY BE USED OUT OF SEASON.

silverbeet (Swiss chard)	600 g (1 lb 5 oz/1/2 bunch)
cavolo nero	1 kg (2 lb 4 oz)
olive oil	60 ml (2 fl oz/1/4 cup)
onions	2, finely chopped
celery	2 stalks, finely chopped
chicken or vegetable stock	3 litres (104 fl oz)
tomato paste (concentrated purée)	2 tablespoons
cayenne pepper	1/4 teaspoon
canned cannellini beans	800 g (1 lb 12 oz), drained
white country-style bread	6-8 thick slices
extra virgin olive oil	to serve

Strip the silverbeet leaves off the stalks, discarding the stalks, to give about 250 g (9 oz) of leaves. Rinse under cold water and shake off the excess. Strip and rinse the cavolo nero leaves in the same way. Shred the silverbeet and the cavolo nero.

Heat the olive oil in a very large saucepan over medium heat. Add the onion and celery and cook for 4-5 minutes. Add the silverbeet and cavolo nero and sauté until wilted. Add the stock and bring to the boil. Stir in the tomato paste. Add the cayenne pepper and season with salt and freshly ground black pepper. Reduce the heat and simmer for 1 hour.

Process half the cannellini beans until smooth. Stir all of the cannellini beans into the pan and simmer for 15 minutes.

Lightly toast the bread and put a slice in each serving bowl. Ladle some soup into the bowls to half fill them and set aside for 1-2 minutes for the toast to soften. Ladle more soup into the bowls and drizzle with extra virgin olive oil. Serve hot.

Cavolo nero simply translates as black cabbage, although this dark green leaf is actually a variety of kale. Tangy and vaguely sweet, cavolo nero is wonderful in a soup with beans and has a natural affinity with pork. The raw leaves are tough, but slow braising will render them meltingly tender. Don't be put off by the dark appearance or unfamiliar name — cavolo nero is utterly simple to prepare and can be used in place of silverbeet, spinach or cabbage. However, unlike those leafy vegetables, it can withstand long cooking and develops a darker colour and more distinct flavour the longer it cooks.

celeriac and carrot
dahl with naan

TO ENSURE A FIRM, UNIFORM FLESH, CHOOSE CELERIAC THAT ARE ABOUT THE SIZE OF A GRAPEFRUIT. THOSE WITH SMOOTHER SURFACES WILL BE EASIER TO PEEL. ONCE PEELED AND EXPOSED TO AIR, THE FLESH WILL DISCOLOUR, SO HAVE A BOWL OF ACIDULATED WATER ON HAND IF THE CUT PIECES ARE NOT TO BE USED IMMEDIATELY.

olive oil	2 tablespoons
yellow mustard seeds	1 teaspoon
onion	1, chopped
garlic	2 cloves, crushed
fresh ginger	1 tablespoon finely grated
cumin seeds	2 teaspoons
ground coriander	1 tablespoon
ground turmeric	1/2 teaspoon
sambal oelek	2 teaspoons
black lentils	375 g (13 oz/1 1/2 cups), rinsed (see note)
celeriac	1 medium, peeled and cut into 2 cm (3/4 inch) chunks
carrots	2, peeled and cut into 2 cm (3/4 inch) chunks
mint	1 handful, coarsely chopped if large
naan	to serve

Heat the olive oil in a large non-aluminium saucepan over low heat and add the mustard seeds. When they start to pop, add the onion, garlic and ginger. Fry for 5 minutes, stirring often. Add the cumin seeds, ground coriander, turmeric and sambal oelek, increase the heat and fry for 1 minute.

Add the lentils, celeriac and carrot and stir to coat. Add 1.5 litres (52 fl oz/6 cups) hot water and bring to the boil. Reduce the heat and simmer for 10 minutes, stirring once or twice. Add more hot water if needed to just cover the lentil mixture. Simmer for 15–20 minutes, or until the vegetables are tender and most of the liquid has been absorbed. Season with salt, to taste, stir through the mint and serve with naan.

Note: black lentils are available from health food shops and speciality food stores as Beluga lentils. If unavailable, use puy lentils instead.

Celeriac, as its name suggests, is a member of the celery family and has a taste reminiscent of both celery and parsley. This versatile root can be used in a recipe in place of celery, or treated as a vegetable in its own right. The skin is fairly inedible and should be removed before use unless you are planning to bake the root whole. The leaves and stalks are useful for assessing freshness (they should be pert and bright) but are inedible and should be removed before you store the celeriac in the fridge. Celeriac is relatively low in carbohydrates and can be used in place of potato for those who are counting grams of carbohydrate.

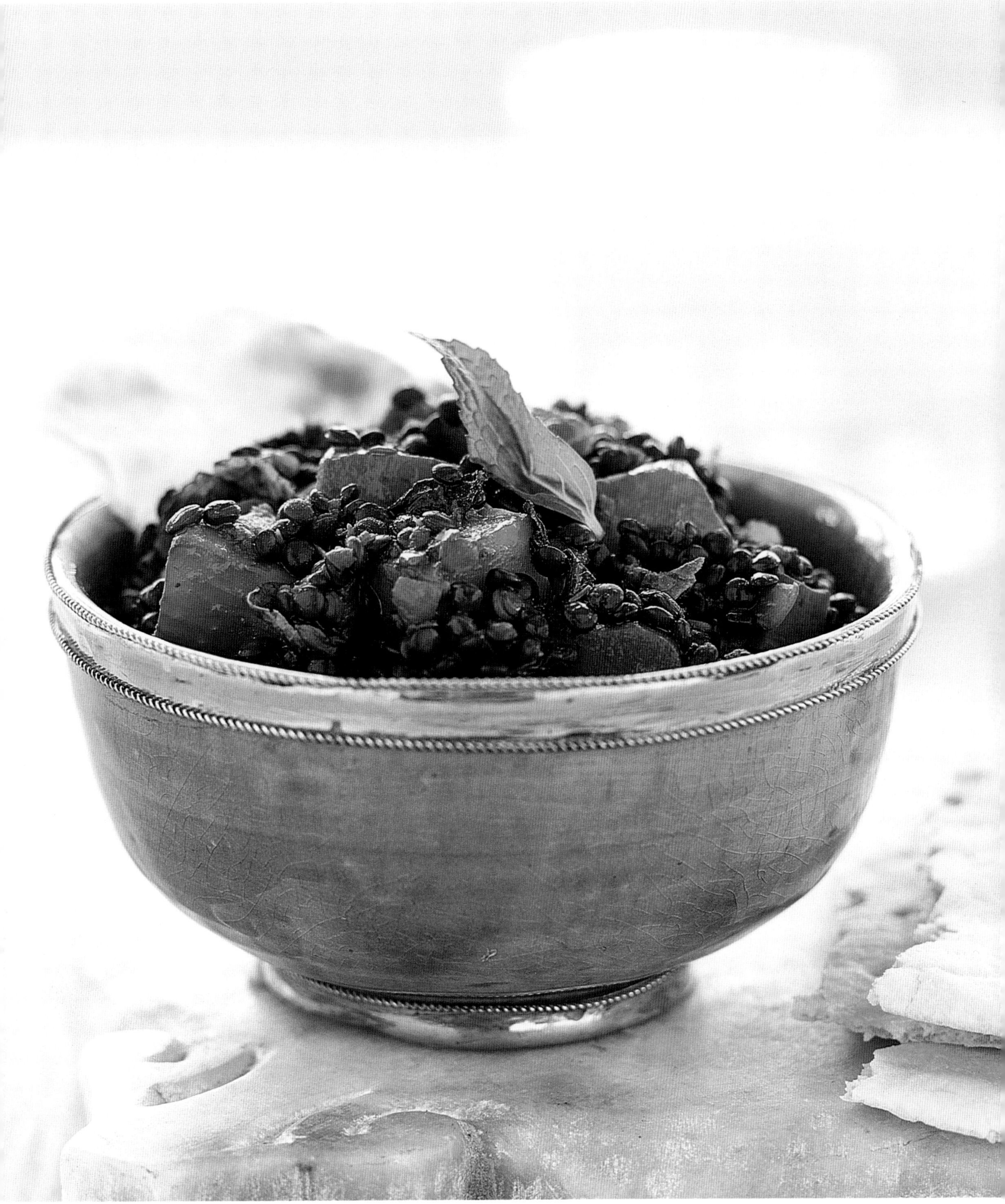

three ways with cabbage

FORGET THE CABBAGE SOUP DIET, PUT AWAY IMAGES OF INSTITUTIONAL COOKING AND REDISCOVER THE TRUE BEAUTY OF THE HUMBLE CABBAGE. MAKE SOMETHING DIFFERENT FOR THE BUFFET WITH THIS SPICY ASIAN COLESLAW. EXPERTS AT MAKING SOMETHING OUT OF NOTHING, THE IRISH INVENTED ONE OF THE MOST DELICIOUS OF WINTER INDULGENCES, COLCANNON. IT'S JUST CABBAGE AND MASH WITH PLENTY OF BUTTER, BUT THE WHOLE IS SO MUCH MORE THAN THE SUM OF ITS PARTS. OR, FOR A TENDER TREAT, BAKE BABY CABBAGES IN BUTTER.

asian-style coleslaw

Combine 200 g (7 oz/2²/₃ cups) finely shredded red cabbage and 175 g (6 oz/2¹/₃ cups) finely shredded Chinese cabbage in a large bowl. Peel 1 large carrot and shave it with a vegetable peeler. Thinly slice 1 small red onion and 1 seeded medium red chilli (optional) lengthways. Add the carrot, onion and chilli to the bowl, along with 80 g (2³/₄ oz/³/₄ cup) thinly sliced snow peas (mangetout), 1 small handful torn Thai (holy) basil and 2 tablespoons coarsely chopped roasted peanuts and toss to combine. To make the dressing, put 2 tablespoons lime juice, 1¹/₂ teaspoons finely grated fresh ginger, 90 g (3¹/₄ oz/¹/₃ cup) light sour cream, 1 teaspoon fish sauce and 1 crushed garlic clove in a small bowl and whisk until combined. Pour over the cabbage mixture and toss well to coat. Scatter 2 tablespoons coarsely chopped roasted peanuts on top. Serve at room temperature. Serves 4.

colcannon

Peel and cube 500 g (1 lb 2 oz) boiling potatoes. Boil in a saucepan of salted water until tender, then drain. Add 40 g (1¹/₂ oz) butter and 60 ml (2 fl oz/¹/₄ cup) milk, and salt and freshly ground black pepper, to taste. Mash until smooth. Heat 40 g (1¹/₂ oz) butter in a frying pan over low heat and fry the white part of 1 sliced leek for 4–5 minutes, or until soft but not brown. Add 400 g (14 oz/ 5¹/₃ cups) shredded curly kale or savoy cabbage and cook, stirring, for 8 minutes, or until softened. Add the potato and a pinch of ground nutmeg and toss to combine. Check the seasoning before serving. Serves 4.

butter baked baby cabbage

Cut 1 baby cabbage (about 500 g/1 lb 2 oz) into 4 wedges and place, cut side up, in a small baking dish. Add 2 tablespoons chicken stock or water. Melt 50 g (1³/₄ oz) butter in a small saucepan and stir in a large pinch each of ground ginger and sweet paprika. Drizzle over the cabbage wedges and place a thyme sprig on each. Bake in a preheated 180°C (350°F/Gas 4) oven for 40 minutes, or until tender and a little crispy around the edges. If not quite cooked, cover with foil and bake for a further 10–15 minutes. Spoon any pan juices over the top for serving. Serves 4.

spiced baby turnips.....................................serves 4

TURNIPS, FOR CENTURIES A EUROPEAN STAPLE, FELL FROM FAVOUR ONCE POTATOES WERE INTRODUCED FROM SOUTH AMERICA. ACCORDING TO TYPE, TURNIPS MAY HAVE WHITE, GREEN OR PURPLISH SKIN. THE FLESH IS USUALLY WHITE. THEY CAN BE EATEN RAW OR COOKED, BUT ARE BEST YOUNG, WHEN THEIR FLAVOUR IS DELICATE.

roma (plum) tomatoes	400 g (14 oz) small
olive oil	60 ml (2 fl oz/1/4 cup)
onions	3 small, sliced
ground coriander	3 teaspoons
sweet paprika	1 teaspoon
baby turnips	350 g (12 oz), trimmed
soft brown sugar	1 teaspoon
parsley	1 handful
silverbeet (Swiss chard)	600 g (1 lb 5 oz/1/2 bunch)

Cut the core from each tomato and score a cross in the base. Place in a heatproof bowl and cover with boiling water. Leave for 30 seconds then transfer to cold water and peel the skin away from the cross. Cut the tomatoes into 1.5 cm (5/8 inch) slices and gently squeeze out most of the juice and seeds.

Heat the olive oil in a large frying pan over medium heat and fry the onion for 5–6 minutes, or until soft. Stir in the coriander and paprika, cook for 1 minute, then add the tomato, turnips, sugar and 80 ml (21/2 fl oz/1/3 cup) hot water. Season well. Cook over medium heat for 5 minutes.

Cover the pan, reduce the heat to low and cook for 4–5 minutes, or until the turnips are tender.

Meanwhile, strip the silverbeet leaves off the stalks, discarding the stalks, to give about 250 g (9 oz) of leaves. Rinse under cold water and shake off the excess.

Stir the parsley and silverbeet into the pan, check the seasoning and cook, covered, for 4 minutes, or until the silverbeet is wilted. Serve hot.

Cut a cross in the base of the tomatoes

After plunging the tomatoes in boiling water, peel off the skin

Squeeze the tomatoes to remove the seeds and excess juice

three ways with potatoes

IS THERE A MORE WIDELY LOVED VEGETABLE THAN THE HUMBLE YET VERSATILE POTATO, OR ONE MORE CAPABLE OF INDUCING A STATE OF MOUTH-WATERING NOSTALGIA? BUT NOW IT'S TIME TO STEP OUTSIDE THE COMFORT ZONE AND DISCOVER WAYS TO REALLY MAKE THIS CUPBOARD STAPLE SING. TRY COOKING SPUDS IN SPARKLING WINE, OR WHIP UP A DIVINE SALAD WITH KIPFLERS, LAMB AND SORREL. AND FOR SOMETHING REALLY DIFFERENT, PAIR PINK FIR POTATOES WITH A SESAME-MISO DRESSING FOR SOME FUSION CUISINE THAT REALLY WORKS.

potatoes cooked in sparkling wine

Using a vegetable peeler, peel off a strip of skin from around the middle of 16 baby red potatoes. Put the potatoes in a saucepan and pour in 750 ml (26 fl oz/3 cups) dry sparkling white wine. Add 3 teaspoons fennel seeds, 2 teaspoons grated lemon zest, 2 bay leaves and a good pinch of salt. Cover partially and bring to the boil over medium–high heat. Simmer for about 30 minutes, until tender when pierced. Drain and transfer to a serving dish. Drizzle with 30 g (1 oz) melted butter and toss gently. Serve hot. Serves 4.

warm salad of kipfler potatoes with lamb and sorrel

Combine 60 ml (2 fl oz/1/4 cup) olive oil, 1 tablespoon white wine vinegar, 2 teaspoons tangerine-infused olive oil and 1 crushed garlic clove in a small pitcher. Season with salt and freshly ground black pepper. Put 250 g (9 oz) lamb backstraps (loin fillet) in a dish and pour in half the dressing. Marinate for 1 hour. Boil 600 g (1 lb 5 oz) peeled kipfler potatoes or anya potatoes for 12–15 minutes, or until just tender, then drain. Grill the lamb on a hot barbecue or chargrill pan for 5 minutes each side, or until medium–rare. Add the potatoes for the last 5 minutes to brown. Remove from the heat and set aside for 2 minutes. Cut the potatoes into chunks and thinly slice the lamb on the diagonal. Put the potatoes and lamb in a bowl with the shredded leaves of 80 g (2³/4 oz/1 bunch) sorrel, 1 small handful torn basil and the remaining dressing. Toss to coat. Serve warm. Serves 4.

pink fir potatoes with sesame miso dressing

Scrub 750 g (1 lb 10 oz) pink fir potatoes. Put the potatoes in a large saucepan of water and bring to the boil. Add 1/2 teaspoon salt, reduce the heat and simmer for 12–15 minutes, or until just tender. Meanwhile, combine 1 1/2 tablespoons each of white miso paste, lime juice, honey and tahini, 1 teaspoon sesame oil, 1 crushed garlic clove and 2 tablespoons water in a large bowl. Drain the potatoes and allow to cool slightly before cutting them into 2–3 cm (³/4–1 1/4 inch) slices on the diagonal. Add to the bowl. Cut 4 spring onions (scallions) into short lengths on the diagonal. Add to the bowl, along with 2 tablespoons roasted peeled pepitas (pumpkin seeds) and 1 small handful mizuna (or combined mint and coriander/cilantro) leaves. Season lightly with sansho pepper, toss to coat and serve immediately. Serves 4.

potatoes cooked in sparkling wine

kohlrabi mash with cider . . . . serves 4

THE EXOTIC-LOOKING KOHLRABI IS A MEMBER OF THE CABBAGE FAMILY, WITH A MILDLY SWEET FLAVOUR AND A DENSE, SOLID FLESH. WHEN FRESH, IT HAS A HARD BODY WITH A SATINY SKIN. PEEL OFF A GOOD 5 MM (1/4 INCH) OF SKIN WHEN PREPARING. ONCE PEELED, KEEP IN ACIDULATED WATER IF NOT COOKING IT IMMEDIATELY.

kohlrabi	600 g (1 lb 5 oz)
apple cider	290 ml (10 fl oz)
potatoes	300 g (10 1/2 oz), peeled and cut into chunks
cream	2 tablespoons

parsley oil

parsley	1 small handful
dijon mustard	1 scant teaspoon
white wine vinegar	1 teaspoon
extra virgin olive oil	125 ml (4 fl oz/1/2 cup)

Thickly peel the kohlrabi, cut it into small dice and put it in a saucepan. Add 250 ml (9 fl oz/1 cup) of the apple cider and 250 ml (9 fl oz/1 cup) water and bring to the boil. Reduce the heat and simmer for 30 minutes. Add the potato and 500 ml (17 fl oz/2 cups) boiling water and simmer for 20 minutes, or until the kohlrabi and potato are very tender, then drain.

Meanwhile, to make the parsley oil, put the parsley, mustard, vinegar and olive oil in a small food processor and process for about 45 seconds, until smooth. Season with salt and freshly ground black pepper.

Purée the kohlrabi and potato using a potato ricer or mouli. Do not use a food processor, which will give too fine a texture and will draw out the starch. Transfer to a bowl and add the cream, remaining apple cider and salt and white pepper, to taste. Mix well. Serve immediately, with the parsley oil drizzled over the top.

Exotic though the name may sound, kohlrabi translates from German to the very mundane 'cabbage turnip'. In fact kohlrabi is a close cousin of the brussels sprout, though it has a mild, sweet taste not dissimilar to a that of turnip. When selecting kohlrabi, look for smaller bulbs with fresh tops and thin rinds, as these will have the sweetest taste and finest texture once cooked. Young kohlrabi are delicious eaten raw and their leaves are fabulous torn and tossed through a stir-fry or salad. Kohlrabi can be stored in the vegetable drawer of the refrigerator for about 3 days.

roast winter vegetables with fresh dates
.... serves 4

THIS COLOURFUL MIX OF FRESH WINTER VEGETABLES HAS A SURPRISING SAVOURY FINISH. IT CAN BE COOKED IN THE SAME ROASTING TIN AS THE JOINT OF MEAT, IF THE TIN IS BIG ENOUGH. TRY VARYING THE VEGETABLES — ROOT VEGETABLES WORK BEST, BUT BRUSSELS SPROUTS AND WEDGES OF BABY CABBAGE ARE ALSO SUITABLE.

pink fir potatoes	450 g (1 lb), scrubbed
carrots	4 small, untrimmed, scrubbed
parsnips	2 small, peeled and halved lengthways
oregano	6 sprigs
olive oil	60 ml (2 fl oz/¼ cup)
French shallots	6, peeled
garlic	2 cloves, thinly sliced
fresh dates	6, pitted and quartered lengthways
extra virgin olive oil	1½ tablespoons
sea salt flakes	to serve

Preheat the oven to 200°C (400°F/Gas 6). Put the potatoes, carrots, parsnips and 4 of the oregano sprigs in a large roasting tin. Add the olive oil and toss to coat. Spread out the vegetables and roast for 20 minutes.

Reduce the heat to 180°C (350°F/Gas 4). Turn the vegetables and add the shallots and garlic. Roast for 30 minutes. Scatter with the dates and roast for a further 10–15 minutes, or until all the vegetables are tender.

Transfer the vegetables to a serving dish. Strip the leaves from the remaining oregano sprigs and add them to the vegetables. Drizzle with the extra virgin olive oil, scatter with sea salt flakes and season with a few good grinds of black pepper. Serve hot.

French shallots (also called eschalots) are one of the smallest members of the onion family and their bulbs are often tinged with purple and divided into bulblets. With a flavour that is somewhere between Spanish onion and garlic, shallots make a tasty base for sauces, pastas, stews and bakes, and also work well tossed raw through a salad. Their papery, copper-hued skins make a great wrapping when roasting them whole, letting them soften and caramelize without burning. When buying, choose specimens that have not begun to sprout, and store as you would onions.

fries

ingredients

More important than the type of potato is its flavour, and that the fries are dry when put into the hot fat. Kipfler, spunta, idaho (russet burbank) and king edward are all good choices. The size doesn't matter, as long as you can cut chips of a good length.

The high temperatures needed to deep-fry successfully require a fat that doesn't smoke or burn at temperatures of 190°C (375°F) or more. Traditionally, suet or lard was used. Both have a high smoking point, but their distinctive flavour is out of favour with today's palates. Some swear by goose fat, but the cost makes this a very special fry! Most vegetable oils fit the bill, and peanut oil is an excellent choice, as its smoking point is well above the temperatures required and the flavour, though mild, is pleasant.

equipment

Ideally, use a heavy-based saucepan of about 20 cm (8 inches) diameter, deeper than it is wide. A removable deep-frying basket makes it easy and safe to lower and lift batches, but beware of those with fine wire, as they can damage the potatoes.

preparation and cooking

Wash and peel the potatoes, then cut them into sticks of about 7.5 x 1 x 1 cm (3 x ½ x ½ inch). Rinse well to get rid of the surface starch. This prevents the chips from sticking together and encourages crispness. Dry thoroughly on paper towels.

Half fill the saucepan with oil and heat to 160°C (315°F). If you don't have a thermometer, dip in a wooden spoon; the fat is hot enough if bubbles rise from the spoon. Alternatively, a cube of bread will brown in 30–35 seconds when dropped in the oil.

Briefly lower the wire basket or utensil to be used into the oil to coat it. This will help prevent sticking. Fry the potatoes in batches to keep the oil temperature constant. Cook them for 4–5 minutes initially; they will come out with just a touch of colour. Drain on paper towels and increase the heat to 190°C (375°F), at which temperature a cube of bread will brown in 10 seconds. Return the potatoes and fry for about 1 minute, until golden brown. Drain on fresh paper towels. If you sprinkle the fries with salt, any excess oil is absorbed and the fries remain crisp.

carrot gingerbread with lemon topping
.... makes an 18 x 11 cm (7 x 4¼ inch) loaf

CARROTS ARE ONE OF THOSE VEGETABLES WHOSE FLAVOUR CHANGES WHEN BAKED, AND WHEN BAKED WITH SUGAR THEY ARE ALMOST UNRECOGNIZABLE. AS A VEGETABLE THEY ARE NOT ALWAYS A FAVOURITE, BUT IT IS HARD TO FIND SOMEBODY WHO DOESN'T LOVE CARROT CAKE.

butter	185 g (6½ oz)
golden syrup or dark corn syrup	175 g (6 oz/½ cup)
light brown sugar	115 g (4 oz/scant ⅔ cup)
carrot	1 large, grated to give 150 g (5½ oz/1 cup)
bicarbonate of soda (baking soda)	1 teaspoon
plain (all-purpose) flour	185 g (6½ oz/1½ cups)
self-raising flour	90 g (3¼ oz/¾ cup)
ground ginger	1¼ tablespoons
mixed spice	1½ teaspoons

lemon glaze

icing (confectioners') sugar	185 g (6½ oz/1½ cups), sifted
butter	5 g (⅛ oz), softened
lemon juice	3 teaspoons

Put the butter, golden syrup, sugar and 125 ml (4 fl oz/½ cup) water in a medium saucepan. Stir over medium heat until the butter has melted and the sugar has dissolved. Slowly bring to the boil, then remove from the heat.

Preheat the oven to 180°C (350°F/Gas 4). Grease an 18 x 11 cm (7 x 4¼ inch) loaf tin and line the base and 2 sides with baking paper. Add the carrot and bicarbonate of soda to the butter mixture, stir well and set aside to cool for 30 minutes.

Sift the flours, ginger and mixed spice into the carrot mixture and beat until smooth. Pour into the tin and bake for 35 minutes, or until a skewer comes out clean when inserted in the middle. Leave in the tin for 5 minutes then turn out onto a wire rack to cool.

To make the lemon glaze, combine the icing sugar, butter and 1 teaspoon of the lemon juice in a bowl. Add more lemon juice to give a stiff paste. Place over a bowl of hot water and stir until spreadable. Cut the cold cake into squares. Using a hot knife, spread with the icing.

Don't be fooled by the common myth that carrots help you see in the dark; although they are high in beta-carotene, there is no proof that they have any effect at all on eyesight. Nor have carrots always been orange. In fact, until they were adapted as a commercial crop, carrots came in red, black, yellow, white and even purple-skinned types with bright yellow flesh. Now you'd be hard pushed to find anything except orange carrots in your local supermarket, but you should be able to find bunches of baby carrots with their frothy tops still attached. Naturally sweet, carrots lend themselves to baked recipes such as cakes and muffins as well as they do to savoury dishes.

potato crepes with berries and mascarpone cream .... serves 4

THESE POTATO-BASED CREPES ARE A GREAT WAY TO USE LEFTOVER MASHED POTATO, BUT THEY CERTAINLY WARRANT STARTING FROM SCRATCH WITH RAW POTATOES. THEY'RE SIMPLE AND DELICIOUS. MULBERRIES OR BOYSENBERRIES, WHEN IN SEASON, MAY BE USED INSTEAD OF BLACKBERRIES.

mascarpone cream

mascarpone cheese	200 g (7 oz/heaped 3/4 cup)
cream (whipping)	60 ml (2 fl oz/1/4 cup)
icing (confectioners') sugar	2 tablespoons
raspberries	150 g (51/2 oz/1 punnet)
blackberries, mulberries or boysenberries	150 g (51/2 oz/1 punnet)
icing (confectioners') sugar	2 tablespoons, plus extra to serve
balsamic vinegar	2 teaspoons
potatoes	250 g (9 oz)
eggs	4, lightly beaten
plain (all-purpose) flour	125 g (41/2 oz/1 cup)
caster (superfine) sugar	2 tablespoons
milk	325 ml (11 fl oz)
canola oil spray	for cooking
icing (confectioners') sugar	for dusting

To make the mascarpone cream, combine the mascarpone, cream and icing sugar in a small bowl.

Put the raspberries and blackberries in a bowl and add the icing sugar and balsamic vinegar. Toss gently to coat.

Peel the potatoes and cut into chunks. Put in a saucepan of boiling water with a pinch of salt and boil for about 20 minutes, until very tender. Drain and mash with a potato ricer or a vegetable masher (do not use a food processor or blender). Transfer to a bowl and gradually stir in the eggs. Sift the flour onto the mixture, add the sugar and stir to combine. Gradually stir in the milk. Add a pinch of salt and set aside for 15 minutes.

Heat a non-stick crepe pan over medium heat and spray lightly with canola oil. Pour 80 ml (21/2 fl oz/1/3 cup) batter into the pan and tilt the pan to spread the batter thinly. Fry for about 40 seconds, until bubbles appear on the surface and the edges are dry, then turn the crepe and cook on the other side for 40 seconds, or until brown. Slide onto a plate. Continue in this way until you have made 8 crepes. (There is enough batter to allow for a couple of trial runs.)

Spoon 1 tablespoon of the mascarpone cream onto one-quarter of each crepe and add some berries. Fold the crepe over once to give a half moon shape, then over again to give a rough triangle. Dust with icing sugar to serve.

Note: If using leftover mashed potato you will need 225 g (8 oz/ 1 cup). If the potato is cold, mix it with the eggs and flour using a hand-held beater to give a smooth batter.

Pour batter into the pan and tilt the pan to spread the batter

Fold the crepe over to enclose the cream mixture and berries

index

Published by Murdoch Books Pty Limited.

Murdoch Books Australia
Pier 8/9, 23 Hickson Road, Millers Point NSW 2000
Phone: +61 (0)2 8220 2000 Fax: +61 (0)2 8220 2558

Murdoch Books UK Limited
Erico House, 6th Floor North, 93–99 Upper Richmond Road
Putney, London SW15 2TG
Phone: + 44 (0) 20 8785 5995 Fax: + 44 (0) 20 8785 5985

Chief Executive: Juliet Rogers
Publisher: Kay Scarlett

Concept and art direction: Vivien Valk
Editorial director: Diana Hill
Designer: Lauren Camilleri
Project manager and editor: Janine Flew
Recipes: Jo Glynn
Text: Francesca Newby
Photographer: Ashley Mackevicius
Stylist: Wendy Berecry
Food preparation: Jo Glynn
Production: Monika Vidovic

National Library of Australia Cataloguing-in-Publication Data
Cooking vegetables.
Includes index.
ISBN 1 74045 469 3
1. Cookery (Vegetables)
641.45

Printed by Toppan Hong Kong in 2005. PRINTED IN CHINA.

IMPORTANT: Those who might be at risk from the effects of salmonella poisoning (the elderly, pregnant women,
young children and those suffering from immune deficiency diseases) should consult their doctor with any
concerns about eating raw eggs.

CONVERSION GUIDE: You may find cooking times vary depending on the oven you are using. For fan-forced
ovens, as a general rule, set the oven temperature to 20°C (70°F) lower than indicated in the recipe. We have
used 20 ml (4 teaspoon) tablespoon measures. If you are using a 15 ml (3 teaspoon) tablespoon, for most
recipes the difference will not be noticeable. However, for recipes using baking powder, gelatine, bicarbonate of
soda, small amounts of flour and cornflour (cornstarch), add an extra teaspoon for each tablespoon specified.